PROVIDING
PRACTICAL SUPPORT
FOR PEOPLE
WITH AUTISM SPECTRUM
DISORDER

of related interest

Asperger's Syndrome
A Guide for Parents and Professionals
Tony Attwood
Foreword by Lorna Wing
ISBN 978 1 85302 577 8

A Self-Determined Future with Asperger Syndrome
Solution Focused Approaches
E. Veronica Bliss and Genevieve Edmonds
Foreword by Bill O'Connell, Director of Training, Focus on Solutions
ISBN 978 1 84310 513 8

Families of Adults with Autism
Stories and Advice for the Next Generation
Edited by Jane Johnson and Anne Van Rensselaer
Foreword by Stephen Edelson, Autism Research Institute, San Diego
ISBN 978 1 84310 885 6

Asperger Syndrome and Employment
Adults Speak Out about Asperger Syndrome
Edited by Genevieve Edmonds and Luke Beardon
ISBN 978 1 84310 648 7
Adults Speak Out about Asperger Syndrome series

Asperger Syndrome and Social Relationships
Adults Speak Out about Asperger Syndrome
Edited by Genevieve Edmonds and Luke Beardon
ISBN 978 1 84310 647 0
Adults Speak Out about Asperger Syndrome series

Autism, Discrimination and the Law
A Quick Guide for Parents, Educators and Employers
James Graham
ISBN 978 1 84310 627 2

Love, Sex and Long-Term Relationships
What People with Asperger Syndrome Really Really Want
Sarah Hendrickx
Foreword by Stephen M. Shore
ISBN 978 1 84310 605 0

PROVIDING PRACTICAL SUPPORT FOR PEOPLE WITH AUTISM SPECTRUM DISORDER

Supported Living in the Community

DENISE EDWARDS

Foreword by E. Veronica Bliss

Jessica Kingsley Publishers
London and Philadelphia

First published in 2008
by Jessica Kingsley Publishers
116 Pentonville Road
London N1 9JB, UK
and
400 Market Street, Suite 400
Philadelphia, PA 19106, USA

www.jkp.com

Library of Congress Cataloging in Publication Data
Edwards, Denise.
 Providing practical support for people with autism spectrum disorder : supported living in
the community / Denise Edwards ; foreword by E. Veronica Bliss.
   p. cm.
 ISBN 978-1-84310-577-0 (pb : alk. paper) 1. Autism--Patients--Care. 2.
Autism--Patients--Services for. I. Title.
 RC553.A88E38 2008
 362.196'85882--dc22

                                            2007044319

British Library Cataloguing in Publication Data
A CIP catalogue record for this book is available from the British Library

ISBN 978 1 84310 577 0

Printed and bound in Great Britain by
Athenaeum Press, Gateshead, Tyne and Wear

Contents

ACKNOWLEDGEMENTS   8
FOREWORD by E. Veronica Bliss   9
INTRODUCTION   11
      Notes regarding definitions and language   14
      Note regarding case studies   14

Part One – The Need for Support

Chapter 1   Philosophy and Principles   17

Chapter 2   Understanding the Nature of Autism Spectrum
            Disorder   22
            Case study 2.1: Matt   26

Part Two – The Nuts and Bolts of Support

Chapter 3   Key Areas for Support   31

Chapter 4   Organization   35
            Instilling order   35
            Managing change   39
            Forward planning   42

Chapter 5   Interpretation   47
            Establishing connections   47
            Maintaining the connections   50

Chapter 6   Communication   52
            Difficulties   52
            Clear communication   54

		Listening	56
		Case study 6.1: Harry	61
		More than words	63
		In all its complexity	65
Chapter 7	Social Interaction		67
		Difference	67
		Coping strategies	70
		Sex	74
		Anti-social behaviour	78
Chapter 8	Health Matters		84
		Physical	84
		Case study 8.1: Mark	86
		Psychological stress	90
		Psychological obsessions	95

Part Three – Implementation and Management of Support

Chapter 9	Managing Support		101
		Planning	101
		The specialist	103
Chapter 10	Care Plan		105
		Design	105
		Implementation	114
Chapter 11	Ethics		119
Chapter 12	Family Support		122
		Caring for the family/carers	122
		Working together	125
		Case study 12.1: Darren	129

Part Four – Support Within Society

Chapter 13	Networks		135
Chapter 14	Disclosure		137
Chapter 15	Education		140
		An integrated society	140
		Opportunities in further and higher education	143

Chapter 16 Employment 146
Finding work 146
Keeping work 148
Case study 16.1: Emma 150

Chapter 17 The Criminal Justice System 153
Victims of crime 153
Arrest 155
Case study 17.1: John 160

Chapter 18 Accessing Services and Benefits 164

Part Five - The Future

Chapter 19 A Vision for Effective Support 171
Surgery 171
Outreach services 172
Emergency support 172
Support in the home 172
Residential support 173
High-level support 174
Support groups 175

Chapter 20 Conclusion 177

APPENDIX 1 180
APPENDIX 2 185
REFERENCES 186
FURTHER READING 187
USEFUL ORGANIZATIONS 189
INDEX 190

Acknowledgements

Together with many people I know who have ASD and their families, I would like to thank the psychologist E. Veronica (Vicky) Bliss. She has worked for many years on a professional and voluntary basis building a high level of expertise in this field. I speak for many when I say I do not know how I would have come through this without her.

Foreword

I have been fortunate, through my work, to meet hundreds of people with autism spectrum disorder (ASD) who have been patient enough to teach me about their own interesting worlds, and I am very pleased indeed to see the publication of this book. In addition to learning from people with autism, I have also read many, many text- and story-books about the 'disorder'. The first thing that absolutely stands out about this book is its very practical description of how life really is for people with autism, and for their families. The author provides a balanced view of disability as present to some extent in everyone, and as only one of the complex facets that make up a person. In this sense, people who have autism are considered as equal, yet both similar and different to people who do not have autism.

The second thing that made me positively howl with appreciation is the way that Denise Edwards so sensibly lays out practical approaches to the development of support services for people with ASD. In my work as a psychologist, I usually get called in to see someone because support services have failed to detect, understand or respond appropriately to a person with very complex needs. This doesn't happen because support services are bad, or because the people don't care. Indeed, people with ASD are often so endearing and support workers get to know them so well that they care very much about those people. What happens is that the 'system' can intervene and insist that one rule will fit all patients/clients. Denise rightly points out that people with ASD are often shaped to fit into 'learning disability' or 'mental health' services, and these services insist that the usual rules of service delivery will apply, even when it is clear that these rules are not helpful to the person with ASD. In addition, because money really does not grow on trees, the support that is commissioned for people is often the one that is cheapest. The author makes a good case to support her statement that 'better quality support often equals less quantity'. Thus, getting the planning, delivery and management of support right by taking in the views of the person with ASD and the people who know him/her well will, in the long run, save spending a lot of money on institutional placements needed when the care package goes wrong.

Third, I love the way that this book emphasizes the importance of listening to people with ASD...*really* listening until your brain seizes and your ears melt (my words, not the author's). This absolutely requires that the listener abandons his/her own framework, expectations and perceptions for interpreting what is heard. It further requires the listener to constantly check that his/her understanding of what is being said is common to both him/her and the person with ASD. From experience, I can guarantee that if a support worker or professional is able to do this, the quality of support for the person with ASD will be very good.

If professionals read and digest this book (and maybe even keep it close to hand) they will be well placed to commission, plan, deliver and manage good quality, practical support for people with ASD. If parents and people with ASD read this book, they may well feel emboldened to think about ways to improve lines of communication or to ask for changes in the way their support is provided. If we can get the support for this group of people right, it will be to the benefit of everyone because the uniqueness and individuality that will be released will put the colour and texture back into our tired old world. I will recommend this book to everyone I see.

E. Veronica Bliss
Director and psychologist, Missing Link Support Services, Ltd

Introduction

At its most prosaic autism is a collection of symptoms as identified by Leo Kanner and Hans Asperger, who each in the 1940s recognized these in their child patients. At its most exotic it has been linked to genius and the 'idiot savant', as publicized by the film *Rainman*. Neither of these encapsulate the day-to-day reality of living with this complex condition. A bland description of a 'social difference' offers little insight into the mayhem it may create in a real-life situation; and whilst many of us will recognize the original thinking and delightful quirkiness of autistic friends, these talents do not avert practical disasters. Both autism and Asperger Syndrome (AS) come under the umbrella term autism spectrum disorder (ASD). It is the aim of this book to outline how best to support people with ASD. It is my intention to look beyond definitions and explore what living with it is like, and how problems can be avoided or negotiated.

To begin from basics, the main characteristics of ASD are:

- *Difficulty in communicating.* People with autism range from being non-verbal to having good language skills. However, all will struggle with spoken communication as they interpret language literally and fail to use or react to non-verbal communication, such as gesture, tone of voice and facial expression. People with Asperger's tend to have better language skills than do those with classic autism.

- *Difficulty in social relationships.* People with autism often appear indifferent to others and uninterested in any social contact. Many, however, particularly people with AS, want to be sociable, but the disability makes it difficult for them to make and maintain relationships.

- *Lack of social imagination.* There is difficulty in the development of interactive imaginative play. People with autism may learn facts, but have problems with abstract thinking. They lack 'theory of mind', which is the ability to understand that each individual has his own mind with his own set of thoughts and emotions. They do not conceptualize that another person thinks differently to them and does not know their thoughts. They do not therefore modify behaviour or speech to accommodate the needs of those around them. The inability to understand the thoughts, feelings and needs of others leads to the extreme difficulties with any social interactions.

I have been to courses, conferences and read books about ASD; however, my knowledge comes mainly from my personal and professional experience with a range of individuals. The simple sentences above explode for me into a million incidences: some amusing, some problematic and some with far-reaching, devastating consequences. My intention in this book is to move from the theory to consider practicalities, and discuss how improvements can be made to the quality of people's daily life. I have seen that ASD affects people of all different abilities, talents and personalities. It is part of their uniqueness and has positive aspects, but in many cases it also means that they need support to cope with daily living Practical methods for doing this form the focus of this writing.

My 25-year-old son, John, was diagnosed as having AS. I have spent a large part of my career working with people with a range of disabilities, such as ASD, dyslexia, Attention Deficit Hyperactivity Disorder (ADHD) and learning difficulties. My interest in working in this field was coincidental, rather than a result of John's difficulties. I had become interested in pupils who did not fit the mould. I was fascinated by finding a way to present material so that the child could learn. I enjoyed the challenge of assisting children to control their behaviour, thus improving their life skills and study habits. I moved from subject teaching to working with pupils with learning difficulties and disabilities. When John was younger I taught for two years in a school for children who were autistic, and then with pupils with a variety of special educational needs in mainstream education. Whilst doing this I returned to university to study for further qualification in special educational needs.

Each person is a unique blend of learning style, personality and much more. The key to providing effective support seemed to me to be to listen carefully to the person, and to apply any relevant theoretical constructs which will assist them in discovering a practical method that works for them. To enhance my skills in doing this, I undertook further study at university and practical training to become a qualified counsellor.

The final stage was to bring together the elements of support for the individual into a structured, deliverable programme. My original subject of study was business, which provided me with a knowledge of systems and management methods. It is vital to any undertaking that all those involved are working cooperatively towards the same goals. The nature of ASD means that consistency is extremely important for those who live with it. Consequently, this has to be developed by ensuring that support requirements, methods of delivery and strategies are communicated to all involved. There then has to be management and overseeing to ensure that support is reliably given, is monitored and adjusted as necessary.

During recent years, I have worked in a college providing tutor support to people with a range of needs including ASD. Outside work, I joined with a group setting up a social club for people with social disabilities. As my son has grown up, I have also moved on to working with adults, so I have progressed through witnessing the effects of ASD at different life stages. Services have developed along the same lines. There is an increase in awareness of autism in children, better diagnosis and more services. The development of services for adults is, however, in its infancy. The aim of this book is to draw together my learning from living and working with people with ASD in order to look at the practicalities of support in the community.

ASD covers a broad spectrum. It will be apparent that support needs differ widely in the amount of hours needed, the type of support and the areas it should focus on. ASD is a complex disorder and it is crucial to have specialist support for it. It is all too easy to draw the wrong conclusion from appearances. An intelligent person who is studying or working and living independently, gives the impression of having no or very minor disabilities. However, ability makes him all too aware of social differences. ASD may be extremely difficult to cope with because the individual recognizes that he does not fit in at social gatherings as he would wish, is not on the same wavelength as colleagues at work and is prone to over-anxiety. Another person may appear more disabled because he has does not have good independent living skills, but may personally not feel so disadvantaged by the condition.

Some people with ASD have developed good coping skills and strategies. Some so much so that they give talks and write about their experiences to help others. For a variety of reasons, others will not manage so well.

Despite the wide disparity in the ways ASD manifests in the accomplishments and behaviour of individuals, the underlying traits leading to diagnosis are obviously common to all. This book will examine practical support methods to address the recognized areas of difficulty with individuals. It will look at services that are needed to meet support requirements, and adjustments that are needed throughout society to provide support for and uphold the rights of those with ASD.

Notes regarding definitions and language

- Autism spectrum disorder (ASD) is used throughout to refer to any disorder that falls within the diagnosis of Asperger Syndrome (AS) or autism.

- Neurotypical (NT) is used to define people who do not have ASD.

- Although ASD affects, and support is given by, those of both sexes, 'he' is used throughout for ease of reading.

Note regarding case studies

Case studies are interspersed throughout the book. These illustrate points regarding support issues covered, although they do not merely fit neatly into the chapter headings. People do not fit into boxes and these personal studies remind us that support is for people. Theoretical knowledge of ASD in the context of this book is important as it gives insight into differences common to those with ASD and suggests effective strategies. Practical support is about far more than this; it is about working with the individual to bring real benefits. The studies not only demonstrate underlying traits and themes, but also show the uniqueness of each person, which influences their lifestyle and support needs.

◆ PART ONE ◆

THE NEED FOR SUPPORT

CHAPTER 1

Philosophy and Principles

It is estimated that around 1 in 100 people live with autism spectrum disorder (ASD). Some are immediately recognized as different, because they appear distinctive, are non-verbal or exhibit unusual behaviours, but most people with ASD look no different to anyone else and respond to language. The core traits are the same for all, but there are marked variations in the way the disorder affects a person. This gives rise to widely differing support needs, as does the individual's circumstances, personality and aspirations.

Every member of society has support from others. It may be informal support from friends and family or it may be professional support, such as from a doctor, teacher, childminder, health visitor or social worker. It may be ongoing over many years, or it may be short term, for example to assist when there is a new baby, when there is illness or to manage a problem at work. Every person is an individual; each with his own life history, unique personality, different abilities and aspirations. What one person finds easy, another will find very difficult. Some people appreciate immediate practical support; others like to look for their own solutions and turn to support with specific problems. Different people need different types of support at different life stages and in varying circumstances.

Giving and receiving support is integral to life within society. We rely daily on the support of others, and often only appreciate this when it is suddenly missing. Someone falls sick or moves away or a professional carer changes jobs, and we realize how vital that person is to us. Many of us think back to difficult times in our lives and say, 'I would not have got through that without a certain person's support.'

The aim of this book is to look at support within this broad definition. The person giving support is anyone who interacts with another person with the intention to assist and provide benefit to him. We each (every member of society – both those with ASD and neurotypicals (NTs)) I hope take on this role at various times in our lives, and also benefit as the recipient of support. Informally support ranges from the long-term care of parents to noticing that another is lost or confused and directing him to the right train. Professionally support is offered by workers, such as teachers, youth workers, careers advisors, medical staff and employers. The majority of these professionals are providing these services generally to any member of the public. In addition to this some professionals, such as psychologists, social workers and professional carers, will provide support specifically to assist an individual because of ASD. This book is addressed to these people too.

Although each person's support needs are unique and individual, there are similarities within certain social groups. As family and friends we will recognize that young mothers appreciate certain types of support, and older people have another set of needs. Professionals are trained to recognize and react to the needs of certain groups, such as adolescents, students or cancer sufferers. It is generally accepted that people who have a disability may need specific support. This book will discuss the broad types of support that can benefit people with ASD. As with any group of people there are themes that run through and ideas that are of use to anyone giving support; however, as in any group each person is an individual, so that support methods have to be selected and tailored to his individual wants and needs.

It is beyond doubt that appropriate support has a major effect on a person's quality of life, and that this in turn dictates the contribution that the individual makes back to society as a whole. The effect is demonstrated dramatically in the remarkable story of Helen Keller. She was believed to be severely mentally disabled, until the person arrived who was able to give the appropriate support to communicate with this blind, deaf girl. Helen was then able to develop as the highly intelligent person she was, going on to receive a university degree and to be an inspiration to many. Stephen Hawking is a brilliant physicist, who is severely physically disabled. He would not have been able to use his exceptional talents to such an extent without the support of carers and his electronic aids.

ASD leads to unusual ways of thinking. This has assisted some to produce outstanding, original work in all fields of science and the arts. However, it also means that those with ASD have difficulty with social relationships and with aspects of everyday living. Giving appropriate support to this group of people relieves the problems they face improving their quality of life, and helps them to achieve their potential which besides giving personal satisfaction has wider benefits for society.

Disability is a negative term, focusing on the ability that an individual lacks. It does not encompass the whole picture – that weakness in one area is frequently balanced by strength in another. A classic example is the blind piano tuner, where the loss of eyesight is complemented by a sharpened sense of hearing. Stephen Hawking might not have developed his intellectual skills to such an extent if he had been physically able and so spent time running round a football pitch. ASD is so complex that aspects of the condition which are disabling are also, paradoxically, strengths. Focusing single-mindedly on one topic may cause problems in everyday situations but be a great advantage in studying or in the workplace. It is not surprising that some people with ASD object to the description of the condition as a disability, but I think it unfortunate if they do not therefore take advantage of available support. *L 215,438*

Temple Grandin, a very remarkable autistic woman, highly regarded in her field of work with animals, acknowledges the role of support, attributing her success to her mother, her therapist, her teacher, and the help she had to develop her strengths and to cope with her weaknesses. I agree with the views of McLoughlin, Leather and Stringer (2002), who assert that focusing on disability can lead abilities to be overlooked, but conversely too much emphasis on talents can mean that difficulties are not addressed which might prevent a person from capitalizing on such talents. They are discussing dyslexia, but I believe the same is true of ASD. 'Disability' is not an adequate term for either of these conditions, because they each encompass strengths and weaknesses. The focus on ASD as a disability will be constructive, however, if it results in support being provided to address the disabling aspects of the condition, so that people can live comfortably within society and achieve their potential.

Any programme of support must be designed to meet the needs of the individual. There is a drive towards greater personalization of health and social services, so that plans are tailored to provide for the person rather than centring on the disability. This policy recognizes the necessity of consulting with the person, and those close to him. Their full involvement from the planning stage is vital. Every person is unique; each has his own preferences, ambitions and wants, with his distinctive requirements for support. Support may be needed generally or to assist in a specific area; it may be for a few hours or many; it may need to be increased at times of stress and decreased as a person grows in confidence. Support requirements are driven by a multiplicity of interacting factors and the nature of these can only be truly understood by the person who lives these daily. What may appear to an outsider as a trivial consideration may be of major importance to the person who is regularly affected by it.

ASD can be an extremely puzzling condition and may appear full of contradictions to those who do not have a full understanding. The most important thing I do when supporting is to listen. What matters is not what I imagine I would want in the circumstances, nor what I believe would benefit a person with ASD, nor what it suits me to deliver. It is rather what meets the needs and desires of the individual, and the only way to know this is to pay careful attention to what he communicates. My role as a professional is to give support to assist the person to develop solutions that work for them. Just as I would do, but in an informal way, for my son if he has a problem. I may offer ideas, but it is for the individual to decide to accept or reject these.

Any person offering support must naturally ensure that there is no risk of harm to the individual or others. Following the aims of the individual means working broadly towards these; it does not mean always agreeing with what he wants in the moment. An aspect of ASD is that people find it difficult to see how their immediate action fits the bigger picture. They may act on an impulse unable to foresee the effects of their action. Planning beforehand, and talking through which actions will promote aims and which will be damaging, means that there can be an agreed strategy in place, so that although the person offering support may advise the individual against doing something or even prevent it, this will be part of a plan devised collaboratively.

Professional support needs to be developed and executed in partnership with people and families. For support to be successful, all concerned need to be aware of its objectives and agree with the plan and strategies involved. Giving support affects the quality of a person's life. If the support is not leading to objectives important to him, or he has no understanding of how it will do so, it becomes an unwelcome intrusion rather than a valuable aid. If the individual can see that it is enabling him towards his objectives, and participates fully, this is empowering. It builds confidence and creates success, which sets up a positive cycle.

In short:

- Every individual needs support.
- The quality of support has a great effect on the person's quality of life.
- Identifying disabilities and giving appropriate support promotes opportunities for talents to be developed.
- People with ASD have many talents.
- Support must be designed around the needs and desires of the individual.
- Professional support needs to be planned and carried out in partnership with the person and family.
- Listening is the most important tool in this process.

CHAPTER 2

Understanding the Nature of Autism Spectrum Disorder

Although all support is individual, those living or working with people with autistism spectrum disorders (ASD) need an understanding of the nature of the disorder. It is often described as a 'hidden' disability. Diagnosis for the condition may be late coming, and is uncertain. One study (National Autistic Society 1999) found that the average age of diagnosis was 5.5 for classic autism and 11 for Asperger Syndrome (AS). Many adults I have met, like the writer Donna Williams, were not diagnosed until adulthood, a few because they recognized autistic traits in themselves. Some people undoubtedly go through their entire life without the condition being acknowledged. Diagnosis involves looking at a cluster of indicators around behaviour and communication. There are internationally recognized classification systems, such as that produced by the World Health Organization, but assessment is not simple and relies on interviewing the person and/or parents/carers/teachers about developments and behaviour.

Awareness has increased rapidly in recent years and yet many people I meet, including professionals in health, education and social services, have little or no knowledge of how ASD may affect a person. Particularly when we see a person who looks ordinary, is living independently and perhaps working or studying, it is difficult to comprehend that they have a disability which has a profound effect on their lives. There are numerous textbook definitions of this disorder, which has an impact on social and communication skills. My aim is to give an up-close and personal description of what it means to live with ASD, as a starting point to develop a background understanding vital to offering support.

John views the world from a different perspective to most people.

If I had in one sentence to sum up the crux of what makes my son different this would be it. John's sight and hearing are within normal ranges, but he does not receive and interpret information in the same way as most people would. This ability to receive data in a different way means that people with ASD may make remarkable achievements in particular areas of study or art, but in everyday life it can create confusion, misunderstanding and the inability to perform what is generally seen as a simple, mundane task.

This is Kanisza's triangle. Most people look at this and see the triangle, but look again: it is not there. All that is on the paper are three 'Pac-Men'. Looking is rarely simply a matter of seeing what is in front of us. As the information comes in our mind makes interpretations and draws conclusions so swiftly that we are unaware it has happened. Jen Birch (2003), who has ASD, describes her horror at seeing 'individuals' top halves were walking in the opposite direction to their bottom halves' (p.33). A reflective surface caused this illusion. She was surprised but stayed calm when she saw half a man on the footpath waving his arms; and was able to figure out that the rest of his torso was in the manhole and simply out of sight. A neurotypical person (NT) makes this leap with no problem.

Communication, communication, communication! The vital element that is at the heart of modern life. Look again at Kanisza's triangle. How can the person who sees the three black shapes on the page understand and communicate with the majority who are talking about a non-existent white triangle? What must he feel as he looks at this picture and hears totally incongruous comments?

I know that the triangle does not exist and the black shapes do. I know because this has been explained to me, and I have the skills to understand this explanation. My mind drew the triangle, so instantly and automatically that it did not occur to me to question its reality myself. If there is to be any understanding of people with ASD, we must first realize that, for any event, there is a possibility of interpretations that are very different to our own. In some countries it is insulting to someone to sit with your feet up, so that the soles of your feet are visible to them. My interpretation is this is a way to relax and the person's feet perhaps ached. It would certainly never have occurred to me as a reason to take offence, had someone not explicitly told me. People's reactions only make sense if we understand the story behind them. The actions of a person with ASD may seem strange, but this is only if we cannot see his perspective.

So the way to change interpretation is by communication. If we wish to explain to the person with ASD the general interpretation that most people would put on a particular situation or action, we need to put this information across to him – except, of course, that communication problems are part of ASD, and so the problems in creating an understanding of the differing perspectives are compounded. It is a complex skill to first recognize that a misunderstanding has been caused by differing interpretations, then clarify it with the individual. The triangle is a simple illusion to explain, but explaining the effect of difference in perception on complex life issues will be much harder. As people with ASD tell their stories, it is obvious that there are reasons for, and meaning to, actions which appear random, odd and inexplicable to NTs on simple observation.

Although I know it is an illusion, I cannot not see the triangle. In practical situations, it seems that people often know the triangle does not exist, but cannot help but respond to it. Feeling stressed and wanting to talk to me, John told his carer to, 'Go away.' It would have been more polite to explain he was worried and would like a private word with his mother. Such things are the Pac-Men that for most people blur into the background. Despite knowing of his communication difficulties and the exacerbating effects of stress, the carer could not remain focused on these, but reverted to seeing the triangle, thus interpreting John's remark as abrupt and evidence of a negative attitude towards him. People have great difficulty holding in mind the nature of the disability and applying this to a situation, rather than staying with the automatic response. ASD is a social disability, and those with it often inadvertently and unwittingly upset others, and have difficulty advocating their needs. The person offering support will be able to develop a better understanding with the individual if he can see beyond a clumsy response.

At a conference about visual impairment some of us were asked to wear a blindfold whilst taking part in a discussion. We found that the blindfolded people made little contribution to the discussion. From personal experience it was hard to join in without the range of visual information I am used to receiving. I could not have imagined how difficult it would be. If I had been asked about situations that I imagined would be tricky for a person with visual impairment, I would not have identified a discussion group. This exercise demonstrates how difficult it is for others to understand the impact of a disability on a person's daily life.

Able-bodied people have spent time in a wheelchair, blindfolded or wearing ear plugs to attempt to have insight into the effects of disability. Such exercises give a minute glimpse at the everyday reality. It is difficult to conceive of a way to simulate ASD. Wearing the blindfold, demonstrated one small aspect, the problem of communicating when you do not pick up information from body language. The closest parallel would perhaps be the experience of being alone in a strange country with little understanding of the local language and customs – *every* day of your life.

To return to my opening statement about my son, ASD is about having a different take on life. It can be frustrating, bewildering and stressful. People have described it as constantly being bombarded by a confusing mass of unrelated happenings. However, it can also be the source of great insight. My son brings to my mind at times the tale of the 'Emperor's clothes'. Whilst the rest of us are reacting to something that is not truly there, he will suddenly point out the simple reality we have missed.

All people are different, but an awareness of underlying ASD traits enhances the ability of someone to offer effective support. This, coupled with careful listening and observation, promotes best practice. Those offering support will benefit from not reaching hasty conclusions, but being willing to acknowledge that there are different ways to interpret any situation or information. As a professional I find this gives fascinating insights and brings rewarding results. As a parent the knowledge that ASD offers an explanation for what otherwise appeared inexplicable, enables me to view my son's difficulties more rationally and feel empowered to better support him.

In short:

- The needs of those with ASD are complex, and not easily identified or understood.

- The different perspective of those with ASD holds both great potential and difficulty.

- Those offering support benefit from being open to the idea that very different perspectives exist.

- The social and communication difficulties inherent in ASD mean that it is difficult for the person to explain his needs.

- Putting aside automatic judgements and seeing remarks or actions in relation to ASD brings greater understanding.

Case study 2.1: Matt

Matt's story told in his own words demonstrates the profound effect that ASD has on the life of a young man who does not have any obvious disability. His parent's recognition of his ASD traits lead to his diagnosis of AS. He has as he says used his diagnosis in a positive way. He benefited from the support of the learning support advisor in his sixth form, and sought out support from the university he attended. Matt has done a great deal to help himself by using his understanding of ASD. He acknowledges, however, that he relies on support from his family and will need professional support in the future. Matt's support profile can be found in Appendix 1.

Matt   *Matt is in the final year of studying for his degree. He is based at home with his parents, but lives independently in residence during term time.*

       Hi, my name is Matt and I was diagnosed with Asperger Syndrome in May 2002 at the age of 18. To be honest I had never heard of the syndrome before September 2001. My parents first suggested the idea of me having some of the symptoms, so that I could search for help to be diagnosed.

       I was born on 16 September 1983 in the Georgian city of Bath in the west of England, and have lived in the Wiltshire town of Devizes for most of my young life. I left home to attend university in 2003 at a town 200 miles from home; it was a hard time in my life, and a major challenge. I think most people with Asperger's find such changes extremely difficult.

As a child I knew that I was different from most of my friends, I struggled with things that they found easy, and I was kind of out of touch with many things socially.

The biggest thing, I guess, that affected me as a child was my inability to keep friends and be one of the crowd. I have always found it difficult in large groups and cannot be the life and soul of the party, so to speak. It was easy to single me out when I was a child, because I had spectacles and was slightly overweight; but there were other reasons that were not clear until the diagnosis. The lack of facial expression was a major reason; who would want to be seen with 'grumpy four-eyes'? The most obvious case of this was a photo taken at the end of my time at school, before sixth form, when we had a friendship group photo. I thought I was smiling, but when the photo was developed, I looked so upset. Why was this? I didn't know and it didn't help when one of my friends said that I had ruined the picture. I felt so low.

The diagnosis was done at my request, because it was an explanation of why I was different, and explained what differences I have from people who don't have Asperger's. In a way my life has changed since May 2002. I can't remember what I was like before the diagnosis. I have used it in a positive way to become more mature, and think about how I behave around my friends. It has gradually helped me socially, because I know what marks me out. I have been able to become socially more aware and now I am one of the group. However, there are still things that I find very difficult, things and that I need help with.

Irrational fears have in a way shaped my life. I used to hate putting my head under the water when having a shower, lighting matches and going on rides at the fair. These are things that most other people take for granted.

Other aspects of Asperger's, that have affected me over the years, are the less obvious internal emotions. Taking things that people say literally is a problem. Misunderstandings arise about what people mean by what they say and how they behave. This has caused me much difficulty over the years, particularly in developing and keeping strong friendships. I have needed the support of my parents, my learning support advisor at sixth form and later at university to help me overcome these problems and difficulties.

My learning support advisor has helped me throughout university in many different situations. First, I have received support regarding the different problems I encounter in my degree programme. This includes interpreting what the question is asking of me, singling out the words that I may misunderstand and which could be at detriment to my answer to the question.

Second, I have received support regarding social issues that affected me whilst at university. Such problems and difficulties as falling out with friends and gauging how my friends are feeling. This caused me much discomfort throughout university, and the support I received was invaluable. Asperger's covers so many different areas, and the assistance I required had to cover so many different things.

I will undoubtedly require some sort of support in the future regarding social issues; just having someone to talk things through with helps so much.

◆ PART TWO ◆

THE NUTS AND BOLTS OF SUPPORT

CHAPTER 3

Key Areas for Support

If it is so complex to identify and meet the needs of an individual with autism spectrum disorder (ASD) where should we begin? The answer as with any support issue must be in listening to the person and, in the case of the professional, also listening to those close to him. An individual may seek support for a specific purpose and have clear ideas of his needs and the objectives. He may for example be seeking help to look for work or to settle into a college course. Others may have difficulty managing all aspects of life, and ASD will complicate the process of recognizing the source of the problem. The difficulties that the user may himself have in identifying and communicating need do not mean that it will be impossible to discover needs and find the appropriate support service, only that it will be challenging and the venture must be entered into with a knowledge that this process is unlikely to be straightforward.

It is useful to consider these broad areas:

- *Organization.* People with ASD, including those who are intelligent and very able in many ways, have difficulty with organizing everyday tasks such as budgeting, travelling independently or managing food preparation.

- *Interpretation.* People with ASD have difficulty understanding and interpreting information that they receive through all senses.

- *Communication.* Some people with ASD are non-verbal; all have some difficulty in using language as a communication tool and will struggle to interpret and use non-verbal forms of communication.

- *Social interaction.* People with ASD have great difficulty in social situations.

- *Health.* ASD can be linked to some physical health problems, such as stomach disorders. Many people are hyper- or hypo-sensitive to sensory input, and unsurprisingly stress is a constant factor for people with ASD.

Support must always have a function, which necessitates providing assistance in these areas. A student may require support with *organization*, not only of notes, but of how to plan the day. He may need support to *interpret* what is meant by an assignment question, or to make sense of what has happened in a situation. He may find it hard to put a point across to the tutor, and need support in this and other areas of *communication*. College or university is an environment where people often expect to make friends and enjoy an active *social* life. This will obviously be challenging for a student with ASD, and it may be vital to provide support in this area to enable the person to be successful. This may be the person's first experience of living away from home, and an individual with ASD is likely to be even less mindful of caring for his *health* than an average student. The move and demands of studying are major challenges, which will increase stress levels.

Other individuals with ASD may require support on a more regular basis and with more practical issues. From the planning stage, all need to be very clear about what the aims and purpose are. The task may be preparing a meal, but everyone involved needs an awareness of why this support is required and what the wider aims are. If we relate meal preparation back to the areas identified above, it involves:

- *Organization.* Preparing a meal involves many skills – deciding what to cook, having the ingredients ready, preparing the correct quantity, having all parts of the meal ready at once – to name but a few.

- *Interpretation.* The person offering support has to pick up and make the person aware of signs that he may miss. For example the instruction may say 'Leave in the oven for half an hour', but if you smell burning before this time is up it is necessary to investigate. If the person is cooking for a guest, it would be helpful to remind him that it is a good idea to check that person's preferences.

- *Communication.* This is the most vital element of any support. Careful listening enables the person offering support to pick up problems experienced or concerns that the person may not make explicit in order to be able to tackle these. The supporter assists by explaining clearly and simply at every stage the reason behind actions.

- *Social interaction.* Whenever people are together there is interaction. The person offering support has the opportunity to model appropriate behaviour. Bearing in mind any particular issues or concerns that have been raised, he can discuss matter arising with the individual, and if necessary with others involved in support.

- *Health.* A good diet naturally forms the basis for good physical health. All of the above work towards giving the individual greater understanding of, and control over, the situation. This builds confidence and help to minimize stress.

The issues involved are complex and the quality of support is extremely important. Families have a wealth of experience, and no one can know more about his support needs than the individual. Combining this with specialist knowledge of ASD can maximize the effectiveness of the efforts of all. This provides the basis for well-designed programmes in conjunction with specially trained staff, who can offer hands-on support or give valuable assistance to those offering informal support. Original models of care in the community were largely designed for physical disabilities, where the aims may be more task orientated. With ASD the need is for the helper to be able to see beyond the task to know how this fits into developing the individual's longer-term aims and ambitions. Doing so promotes effective support, which is invaluable in improving the individual's ability to live, work and socialize.

For someone with ASD having a professional support worker around can in itself be stressful. Living with John when he had carers every day was hard for me, even though I usually only saw the staff at the beginning and end of the shift. It is invasive to have people in the home. Most people find that it is wearing having workmen around for days; even when guests leave at the end of an enjoyable visit, it is good to have your own space back. So imagine what it is like to have a carer there for long hours; now think again and imagine the unimaginable (if you are a neurotypical person (NT)) –

imagine you are in this situation but have ASD. This context makes it imperative that hours support workers put in are purposeful and effective.

High-quality support from specialist professionals may be costly initially, but it is the most beneficial and economical solution overall. An intelligent young woman I know became so depressed that she attempted suicide. She had repeatedly asked for support and was now given someone who would 'pop in for a daily chat'. This addressed none of the issues concerning her, such as not being able to organize her fridge, losing jobs because of her lack of social skills or being isolated in her flat. Instead, she worried about having to be in when this person called, and what she was supposed to talk about. Her requirement is for a specialist who can plan with her to address her needs.

Like many things the better the quality the less the quantity that is needed. The ultimate aim of support should be to improve skills and develop strategies to enable the person with ASD to feel in control and better able to cope independently. Monitoring of progress towards appropriately set goals ensures that support works with the person to develop to their potential. Although more expensive initially, properly directed support is not only beneficial for the individual, but cost-effective in the longer term. Monitoring will ensure that support continues to be constructive and adapts to changing situations and needs.

In short:

- Broad areas for support are organization, interpretation, communication, social interaction and health management.

- Support is complex and specialist management of professional support is essential.

- Quality of support is as, if not more, important than quantity.

CHAPTER 4

Organization

Instilling order

> Reality to an autistic person is a confusing mass of events, people, places, sounds and sights. There seem to be no clear boundaries, order or meaning to anything. A large part of my life is spent just trying to work out the pattern behind everything.
>
> (Description given by an unnamed
> autistic person on the NAS website)

If life is confusing, support needs to bring some order. The difficulties that a person presents with when seeking support are liable to be multiple, complex and bewildering. A good starting point in delivering support for anyone with autism spectrum disorder (ASD) is in assisting him to create structure in his daily living. Liane Holliday Willey in her autobiography describes how order and predictability bring solace and security (Holliday Willey 1999). Faced with a chaotic lifestyle and distress, it is easy to overlook matters which may be considered mundane. The fact is that extremely able people with ASD frequently struggle with day-to-day life skills. Very intelligent students cannot organize themselves to launder their clothes, and may get up to find they are all dirty or still wet in the machine from several days ago. This is one of those superficially trivial things that can be a major problem to the person it repeatedly happens to.

On a practical domestic front, what may be a massive difficulty for a person with ASD, may be an easily solved problem for someone without it. My student may have me totally at a loss when he is absorbed in his subject, but I can work out a routine for ensuring his washing is done on a regular basis. He identified the difficulty, I suggested solutions and he accepted the one that met his needs. Improving daily living skills has benefits in itself in establishing healthy lifestyles, and in pre-empting problems. It is no fun to arrive home tired to find all the food in the fridge is out of date, or to leave the house with no money for your bus fare. Having these things happen on a regular basis and feeling powerless to change matters is unbelievably frustrating, so finding ways to manage daily living has great benefits in decreasing stress levels.

People with ASD like to have regular routines. The ability to adhere to routine is an advantage in many situations, and this skill can be used productively. Structure and organization can be brought to running the household. As a plan is constructed, problems can be considered and systems put in place to deal with them. A planning session when the individual collaborates with support to work out a weekly menu and the necessary shopping plan, gives the person more autonomy, than having someone turn up to go shopping or cook with them. Having someone alongside is sometimes necessary, but has the disadvantage of creating dependence. The individual is empowered instead by being facilitated to complete tasks independently. Planners, charts and checklists are useful in charting progress. Having visual planners or checklists provides security so the person is certain that he is on track with the agreed aims. Consulting it gives a sense of achievement, in showing clearly what has been done. Even a person who has full-time care has a degree of autonomy if he participates in planning, and monitors the results himself.

We all have habitual ways of doing things, and I suspect we do not realize how we cling to these until there is an attempt to change them. Routine is the bread and butter of our daily life. The manager of John's care team related using the ploy of asking people to write down the pattern of their morning activities when they got up out of bed at the start of the day. These were then mixed up, randomly re-distributed and each person asked to use the new routine they received the next day. This is the point when people discover how attached they are to their own habits.

A friend with ASD likes to visit the nearby towns, and in each he has his established route of shops and eating place. He is upset if he cannot sit in his usual place, and order his usual meal. Is this unusual? Many people habitually sit in a particular seat in the café, bar or staffroom, and feel discomfited if they have to sit elsewhere. Some of the traits associated with autism are not as far removed from the norm as they at first appear. People like to holiday, and yet are often heard to say after a break that it is good to be back in routine. Routine is a comfort zone that all humans seek out, and which those with ASD particularly value. Creating ritual and routine, ordering objects and following strict patterns are a feature of ASD. Such routines can appear meaningless and odd, but it is not surprising, when we consider how difficult it is for those with ASD to understand the world, that they try to impose some sense into it. This trait can be employed productively to establish rituals that facilitate daily living, making life more comfortable and less stressful.

A regular lifestyle has a great part to play in maintaining mental and physical health. Disrupted sleep patterns are often a feature of the onset of mental health difficulties, whereas regular regimes of sleep, food and exercise maintain overall health. People with ASD tend to suffer from stomach problems, so it is particularly beneficial to have measures in place to ensure a good diet. As the mother of four young children, my life was made easier by routines, which preserved my sanity and kept me confident that the children had a balanced diet and sufficient sleep.

Bringing order to daily life helps to give an element of predictability and make the chaos around more comprehensible. My son will become disturbed if his surroundings are disorderly. A tidy desk/room/house is proverbially a reflection of a tidy mind. Still and orderly surroundings have a calming effect. Some people with ASD keep their homes very tidy, others do not. As friend with ASD said, 'I hate my room to be a mess, but I don't know how to tidy it up.'

Although John likes order, he does himself create disarray. To 'tidy up' he will bundle everything into the nearest cupboards, and then be dismayed when they fall out on him the next time he opens the door. Life is full of booby traps! He will 'bung' things out of sight and then be angry that he cannot find them. It is supportive to help people to stay ahead of the game by maintaining order. In practical terms this may mean giving support to put things away correctly, to sort cupboards out regularly and ensuring that there is a regular place to keep important things so they do not go missing.

Organization is a good starting point in providing support, because it is non-threatening. Beginning by asking someone dealing with a 'confusing mass' to explain their support needs is only likely to add to their distress. Looking instead at the practicalities of what they do during the day, and establishing a pattern to this, diffuses some of the stress.

It is vital that the professional support worker is willing to engage with the daily life of the person being supported and to see what is important from their perception. As I mentioned before, being bound by habit is not an exclusively autistic trait. It is not easy for us as professionals to change from an established practice. John's support workers tended to adhere to their usual method of cooking on the hob, rather than doing vegetables in the microwave as he normally did. Microwaving is much easier for him as the vegetables do not need draining, but, far more importantly, there is no danger of the pan either boiling over or boiling dry. Support works best when others come into the world of the individual they work with and learn how to do things in the optimum way for him. It is confusing to the person if they use a method he is unfamiliar with, and it takes away his independence. Cooking in the microwave is a method which makes it much easier for John to manage unsupported. It is a skill to select and suggest methods for a simple task, which will eventually allow the person to complete it independently. New technology brings opportunities for improvements in support as in many other fields.

Routine and structure are powerful tools for creating calm and reduce stress. Darren's mother will tell in Case study 12.1 how loss of structure in his life once he left organized education contributed to a decline into unmanageable behaviour. Organization is a good starting point for support, because it can quickly bring about some change. A visible improvement, and one which the person is instrumental in bringing about, boosts confidence and self-esteem. The world becomes more steady and progress on other fronts is possible.

There are, however, two sides to any coin, and blind adherence to habit is not always productive. How many good ideas are rejected simply because we have always done something this way? Regular reviews ensure that routines continue to be appropriate and effective.

At its most extreme, clinging to routine can become disabling as for those with obsessive compulsive disorder (OCD), for whom the need to perform the rituals interferes with normal living. It must be borne in mind that the routines are only the supports; they are only a vehicle and developing and tinkering with them should not become the end in itself, so that the journey is forgotten.

For my son a basic routine gives him something on which to hang his understanding of the world. Routines set up for managing daily activities are a framework from which an individual can begin to give meaning to the multifaceted, rich variety of happenings in everyday life.

In short:

- Organization of routines for daily living is a useful starting point.

- Orderly surroundings help to promote calm.

- Practical benefits are daily living skills are improved and domestic problems pre-empted.

- Health benefits from regular routines.

- These benefits decrease stress, promote self-esteem and increase confidence.

- The best support methods promote independence.

- Those offering support need to be alert to the danger of routine becoming obsession for the person with ASD, or from becoming too attached to the minutiae of these themselves.

- Routines are only the beginning.

Managing change

All change produces stress; even pleasurable change, such as going on holiday, increases stress levels. Change is divided into two categories; that which we expect (perhaps instigate) and can plan for, and that which is unexpected. It is invariably difficult for those with ASD to cope with. In Case study 2.1 Matt acknowledges that, despite wanting it, the move to university was particularly difficult for him, and that change is something that people with ASD generally find challenging. Change is, however, inevitable, as no day is ever the same as the previous one.

Small changes may be imperceptible to most people, but major to someone with ASD. If dinner is at six o'clock and eaten at the table, this should be so. John can cope with, even enjoy, the occasional change if he is prepared for it. He loves to have company, or will especially look forward to eating out. He will find it hard if meal times are frequently haphazard or are taken in front of the TV and so on.

ASD thinking can be wonderfully precise, and also inflexible. Order is kept or it is not. If John is weighing 50g of breakfast cereal for breakfast, it must be 50g. There is no leeway to reason that, say, 45–55g is OK, whereas 200g is not. If whoever is with him says to him 51g is fine, he will see no reason why he should not have 200g next time. John is concerned about details that many people may not notice. He was agitated about changes to the staff rota for his support workers, which is understandable, but his concerns were also around the fact that these led to crossings out and the timetable then looked untidy. His anxiety level was reduced by producing this on the word processor, re-editing it and printing a new pristine version.

Most people instigate minor changes easily. It may be more convenient to vary a normal routine on a particular day, even pleasurable. I might decide that as it is a sunny day I will go out, and do the housework in the evening. As a supporter for someone with ASD it is vital to remember, that he will not have the flexibility of thought that people generally have and so may need routines to be more stringently adhered to. Such a simple adjustment may not be easy, and it may be preferable to stay with the usual unless there is a strong argument for change. The world becomes easier to interpret if as much as possible is held constant.

I think the reason for the panic around change may lie in the person's fragmented view of the world, and in their inability to recognize a similar situation. In practice I see that change is easier for a person to handle, if what remains the same is explicitly pointed out to him. So if John is concerned because he will have a different support worker on shift, it helps to go through what is the same. I explain that he will arrive at the same time as usual, and go through with John what the routine is for the day making it clear that this will stay the same. We are then able to look at the change in this context. It may be that there are then benefits that can be highlighted. A student with ASD, worried at the change of a lecture time, was able once he saw the constants to recognize that this was in fact more convenient for him.

Change is easier to manage if we know it is coming. The better prepared someone is for a change, generally the easier it is to cope. For people with ASD, it helps if the preparation can be as concrete as possible. So if they are beginning college, spending time walking around the campus, practising routines for using the canteen, sitting in the lecture theatre, looking at the timetable and checking the route from one room to the next can be as important as collecting information about the course. It is good to meet tutors to get used to their presence, their mannerisms and the sound of their voice. It is all about having a sense of the new situation so that there is not a sudden bombardment of unusual input. Remember too to look for constants. Even with a major change they are there. As preparations are made for full-time paid workers to take over my son's support, I talk to him about things we do together that we will continue to do.

Unplanned change is harder to cope with. Sometimes it can be pleasant, such as an opportunity to do something you have always been interested in, but even so the person with ASD may prefer his routine. I found out the day before it happened that there was an open day at the local college. John wants to do a course next year and an added incentive to go was that a DJ from the local radio station (a major interest for him) would be there. Despite this he did not wish to change from his routine at such short notice. Handy hint – never throw a surprise party for a friend with ASD!

Unexpected events, even minor, can be very difficult to cope with. I left a teenager to make a regular bus journey back to school. When he did not arrive I went looking and found him still waiting at the bus stop. Although there was no traffic on the normally busy road, he had not looked for an explanation. He did not realize that the road was closed and that he needed to walk round the corner to catch the re-routed bus. Thought processes for a person with ASD can be inflexible and an intelligent person may be incapable of dealing with something that most neuortypicals (NTs) would take in their stride.

Which leads on to contingency plans. Our contingency plan for this pupil was that if the bus did not arrive precisely on time he must stay and wait. Contingency plans are useful. We imagined that if the bus did not come on time, he might be upset and leave the bus stop, so we had discussed with him why it might be late or cancelled. It is always good when planning a new venture to consider what might happen, and to consider it in relation to ASD. Whereas most people are annoyed or impatient if a bus is late, it can be a big deal for someone with ASD that it has not arrived as shown on the timetable. The problem, as you will have noted, is that it is impossible to cover all eventualities. We had not considered the possibility of the bus being cancelled or re-routed. Our plan, however, worked to the extent that the pupil did not wander off and so was quickly found. I wonder how long he would have waited.

Small changes, that may even pass unremarked or cause minor pleasure or annoyance for most, can be very unsettling for a person with ASD and may cause marked differences in his behaviour. It is vital to bear in mind how disturbing seemingly minor changes can be. Some unexpected events or changes are unpleasant, even traumatic, for all. This is when individuals who are not receiving professional support are very much at risk. It is not only that they have to cope with the negative change, but events such as accident, illness and bereavement will affect those close to them who normally help out, and so their informal support system may collapse or may not function as well as usual, just when it is needed most.

Anyone coming in to offer support at crisis point needs to be very aware that the person's behaviour at this time may not be typical of his usual demeanour. It is important to find out how the person usually acts on a regular day, rather than make hasty judgements based on how he presents then. An overreaction by the person offering support, may lead him to impulsively initiate major changes, causing further distress to the person he seeks to assist and starting a downward spiral with serious long-term effects. The first step is to instil some order. At times of crisis we make a cup of tea. This is banal, but true. It is something we can do and it is a familiar, comforting ritual. Rather than taking any extreme measures, the best thing to do is to help the individual get back to normal daily routines, or as close as possible to them, and to concentrate on some practical tasks. A familiar, repetitive, mundane activity can distract and soothe. People with ASD do, of course, need to come to terms with difficult events as we all do, but it takes them longer to process what has happened. The best starting point is to give them a secure base to do this from, by maintaining regular patterns; and then offering space to talk as needed.

Change is the way of the world. All progress is change and it is a positive force. Those offering support need only to be aware of its impact and the need for management.

In short:

- Vigilance is needed to be aware of change.

- The person offering support may need to think 'outside of the box' to realize what is causing agitation.

- When there is change, it helps to point out the constants.

- Being proactive in planning for change pre-empts problems.

- Preparation should be as practical and concrete as possible.

- Contingency plans should be in place.

- In a crisis the best way to restore calm is by re-establishing familiar patterns.

Forward planning

Envisaging options in order to make long-term plans is not easy for anyone, and is even harder for those with ASD. If they struggle to interpret the world that exists around them, then how are they to envisage a future project?

The first stage of planning is to make a choice of direction. A person with ASD will often dwell on a problem. They will go over and over the options, and appear to insistently repeat themselves. The person offering support needs to first appreciate how immensely difficult decision-making can be. The individual being supported will need patience and time to allow him to express his thoughts. However, there is a point where it is helpful to take practical steps to move the person on. Making the situation concrete, practical and visual assists the decision-making process. The options can be drawn up on a sheet of paper. The advantages and disadvantages of each can then be discussed. This gives concrete matters to focus on. It is not only assisting the decision-making process, but it reduces the confusing mass of data to be considered down to manageable chunks. For example for the student considering what seem to be two totally different options of university, it can be broken into comparable points, such as the components of the course, the travelling distance from home and the social facilities. The analysis may throw up a clear result, say that most things are equal and that the decision really rests on the fact that one has a smaller campus that the student is happy with. Keeping an open mind to the awareness that a person with ASD may have different priorities to most people is essential. Whilst course-related factors may be deciding for many students, factors that create an ASD-friendly environment may be of paramount importance. A balance must be struck between listening and giving space, and assisting the person to a decision. Uncertainty is very hard for someone with ASD to cope with, and if this continues it can lead to depression, so efforts should be made to ensure that the process is not unduly prolonged.

People with ASD are impulsive and a decision can change from day to day depending on which piece of information comes to the fore at the time. When my son was detained in hospital many miles from home, he was desperate to return to his house. However, he walked into an important meeting to review the plans for his release, saying adamantly that he wished to remain and settle in that part of the country. The reason was that he had just seen my mother, who lived nearby, so what was uppermost in his mind was the desire to see more of his nan. All the overwhelming reasons for returning to his local area – family, friends, familiarity with the area – were forgotten. Nor did he take into account the practicalities of living near his grandmother. Fond as she is of him, she was horrified by his announcement. Although fit, she is finding it more difficult to be as active as she was, is not getting any younger and was anxious that she would have been unable to offer him any support.

I am always very concerned about influencing my son's decisions. Donna Williams (1992) in her autobiography describes moving in with a boyfriend simply because he asked her to. People with ASD describe finding they are the scapegoat when they have unthinkingly followed others. They are extremely susceptible to being led, and I am conscious of how easily I could influence John's judgement. However, when a major decision is to be made, those offering support can try to ensure that it takes into account the individual's overall needs, and so can question a choice that is made on impulse and in conflict with the individual's usual desires.

Clearly any adult has the right to make choices about how to live his life, provided that choice falls within the law. Still, there are occasions when a person may need others to guide or even take responsibility for a decision. If it is a complex choice with many factors to take into account, some will simply be overwhelmed by the jumbled mass of information presented, and find the decision-making process too stressful. There are ethical considerations involved in needing to ensure that a person's right to choose is balanced against society's responsibility to protect those who are vulnerable. Choice is a privilege, but it brings responsibility and pressure. Clearly we should support people to make their decisions and follow their choices in life. However, we have a duty of care to assist when the demands of making a decision may be overtaxing and is leading to anxiety-related problems, or when an option is detrimental to the person's well-being.

There are on rare occasions decisions that are so complex that they may be better made for the person, but judging that this is such an occasion must be done with a great deal of care. Professionals and family considered the question of where John would live since it was a very difficult decision for my son to make. It was accepted that he would move into a flat selected by the support agency. Plans were made with him on this basis for many months and it was only weeks before the anticipated move that I saw the property. The kitchen was within the small living area, making it wholly unsuitable: anyone with ASD would be unable to cope with such sensory overload. It was particularly unsuitable for John as he cannot mange small spaces, and struggles to control his diet. Having to change plans at this point was traumatic. If we had gone through a proper decision-making process with him considering all aspects of the flat, this situation would not have arisen.

There are complex questions around decision-making, but no matter how hard it is to make a choice, a person has a right to do so. With hindsight, it was wrong to take this choice away from John, by presenting the flat as a definite rather than as an option. At a time when a choice which is likely to be difficult is to be made, sensitive support from a specialist counsellor needs to be provided. This role must be taken by someone who has no interest in the outcome. It is often assumed that any professional will be neutral, but lifestyle decisions will affect staff providing daily support and may have knock-on effects for management. The more vulnerable the person is, the more hours' support he should have and, therefore, the greater the impact of his decisions will be on workers.

The views of those closest to the person and the history of what has happened in similar situations should be investigated, so that these factors can be explored. The person supporting the decision-making process needs to be someone who has specialist knowledge of the way that ASD is likely to affect a person, and who is able to put aside personal preconceptions to truly listen. There is a need to reach decisions as quickly as possible to reduce worry, but this should not be done so hastily that the decisions are not properly thought through.

Once a course of action is decided on, assistance will be needed with the sequencing and logistics of carrying through the plan. A characteristic of ASD is single-mindedness of purpose, and the impulse is often to begin immediately. A student with a pressing question to ask will have no inhibitions about immediately seeking out the tutor and interrupting whatever he is doing. As a starting point, to assure the person with ASD that the course of action will happen, something should be done immediately even if it is only writing or drawing the main outline.

The aspects of forward planning can be incredibly challenging for a person with ASD, regardless of their intellectual level. A visual planner puts stages within a structured time frame. Gantt charts show a time scale on the horizontal axis, and list a breakdown of tasks to complete a project, charting the timing of each (see examples in Appendix 2). This is a technique that is used in work settings, but it is useful for retaining structure in any task. It can be used for anything from planning a day out, to decorating a room, to applying for work. It is again about creating order in a confusing mass of events. The person with ASD will have difficulty holding a sequence of events in mind. A concrete visual reminder is a tool for him to use independently or with support as a coping strategy. Marking off stages makes clear that, although he may not yet have the result he wants, he is making definite progress towards it.

The plan creates stability and holds the frame steady, but it has to be balanced against some flexibility. The future is not predictable, and any number of events can intervene to wreck our carefully made strategy. Some options and variations can be written in, but as previously seen, all possibilities cannot be foreseen. Hard as it is to get across the message, reminders must be given that adjustments may be needed so that it is not too much of a shock if this proves to be the case.

In short:

- All people have a right to choice, and those with ASD may need support to exercise this.

- Support to make decisions needs to be given by a person who has no involvement in daily care.

- Support should be given by someone with counselling skills and a knowledge of ASD.

- The views of those close to the person and history should be reviewed with the person in assisting him to a decision.

- Any project is more manageable for a person with ASD if it is carefully planned and structured.

- Allowances must be made for variables, wherever possible, and reminders given that adjustments may be needed.

CHAPTER 5

Interpretation

Establishing connections

For people with autism spectrum disorder (ASD) this world is a fragmented, disjointed place. A student may have a plan of the campus and a timetable, but marrying up the information on the two and being able to arrive at the correct time and place for a lecture can be a conundrum for even the most able. I often think that ASD is the source of the stereotype of the 'absent-minded professor'. The supporter stands in the role of interpreter exploring with the person to discover the root of difficulties, explaining possible solutions and finding out which works best for that individual.

My son needs continuous interpretation of what is happening and ongoing explanation of the reason for following a path of action. Much of what we do as adults is carried out for our future benefit. We may wash and iron clothes to wear during the coming week. We go to work today for money we will not receive until the end of the month. We may save some of that money, so that there is no benefit until we go on holiday many months later. As people with ASD have great difficulty seeing consequences or planning ahead, they may find it hard to become motivated if the gratification is not instant. Things have to be broken down and explained in a practical way.

For example, I might say to John, 'Iron this shirt and hang it up. On Friday you can put it on and look good for the disco.'

If he is not persuaded, I simply point out the disadvantages of the other option: 'On Friday you will be unhappy if you do not have a smart shirt to wear.'

And then return to the positive option. The final coup de grace is to point out to him on Friday that he looks great and this is because he ironed the shirt on Tuesday. It is all about giving meaning and developing a sense of consequences.

People with ASD often are able to see an exciting different perspective, but totally overlook things that are apparent to most. Often the reason for doing something is so obvious to us that we do not bother to talk about (or even consider) why we do it. Most people at some point complain about going to work, but we also in the main recognize the need to attend! The advantages of having a salary are all too obvious, and there may be other benefits such as job satisfaction or the company of colleagues. The difficulty for a person with ASD is that the mind will be firmly focused on an instantly preferable activity, such as simply staying home listening to music, and none of the wider implications occur to him. Only after a while does it sink in that this activity, which gave instant gratification, is not fulfilling long-term needs.

The person with ASD requires constant reminders of how actions fit into the bigger picture. Some of the work I do is on supply, and as no work means no pay I have a motive for being glad when it is on offer. So I can happily and honestly say to my son, 'Yes, it would have been nice to stay in bed this morning, but aren't we both lucky that we have work and so will have some money to spend next week.'

Some things that people with ASD do can appear pointless to us. Imagine how we would feel if we were told that you had to spend an hour laying pencils in a straight line, or we had to type a list of CDs and another tomorrow, and the next day, the next and the next. I cannot understand why John thinks it vitally important to type up lists and lists of CDs, or why he enjoys flicking switches. Why then should he understand why I ask him to vacuum the carpet? The supporter can help greatly by paying attention to the task at hand, thinking through why it is being done, and relating this to the person he is working with.

It is the role of the supporter to facilitate understanding of this crazy neurotypical (NT) world. He needs to be very clear himself what he is doing and why, so that the person can rely on him to give necessary information, and give it simply and accurately. The most mundane of tasks may need explanation and guidance. John always appreciates the obvious being made explicit. He likes someone to explain to him precisely what needs doing and why it needs doing, and to give feedback. Dave is his favourite support worker when there is housework to be done. He was articulate in explaining that this is because Dave stays alongside John and details exactly what should be done. It is supportive for someone to say, 'This is dirty,' pointing out where there are marks here to remove – and afterwards to reinforce with such comments as, 'Those black patches are gone. That looks much better.' Without such comments John goes through the motions, but does not really get the point. When it is spelt out to him, he is happy that he has achieved something.

Consistently remembering to give an explanation has a great impact on motivation and willingness. It means being pedantic! As the shopping is loaded into the car boot, and I remind that heavy cans and bottles go in first with light, crushable items, such as bread and fruit, on top; the apparently obvious reasons for this are reiterated – yet again.

Children go through a stage where they seem to be forever saying, 'Why?' My son asks this question often, as do others I know who have ASD. Some ask hesitantly, because they have realized that other people do not need to. Attention to detail and explanation at every stage fills in some of the blanks. Many jobs are humdrum and boring, but imagine how much worse they would appear if we could see no object at all to doing them. Supplying an explanation is a small thing, but often small things are what make the difference. A person is likely to respond far better to, 'Let's sweep this mess up. If we do not it will spread and you will have a lot of cleaning to do tomorrow', than he would to simply being told the mess needed cleaning up. Anyone is more willing to do something if he sees a reason for it and a benefit to doing it. Most people will not even consider the reason many jobs are carried out, because it is so apparent. The ASD perspective though is radically different from most people's.

Just as an aside I have gained a great deal from this personally. Looking for a reason to explain to John makes me look again at things I do habitually. Sometimes happily I realize that I don't really have to do it at all. But above all, it is a reminder that even when I am doing something I do not particularly like, there is a worse option which I have rejected in favour of doing this.

In short:

- The person offering support needs to work with the individual to discover what is required, and then be able to interpret the situation and feed back possible solutions.

- For any circumstance, the supporter needs to be clear in his own mind why this course of action should be followed.

- He cannot take it for granted that the reasons for an action have been understood, but must make these explicit and reiterate them to maintain motivation.

Maintaining the connections

The paradoxical nature of ASD is demonstrated again in attention span. The person will be absolutely absorbed, blocking out the rest of the world, when he is engrossed in something of particular interest; but at other times his attention span can be low. Most people will recognize the experience of being called away to answer a phone call, or speaking to a visitor and completely forgetting that they were in the middle of doing something. This distractibility is a common experience for those with ASD. Donna Williams (1994) describes how on the bus journey from one airport to the next, she is distracted when someone mentions an interesting art gallery, goes to investigate and almost misses the next flight.

A person with ASD generally needs to give undivided attention to the task in hand, although it is well within his capabilities. Often we NTs deliberately distract ourselves from boring jobs, watching TV as we iron or listening to the radio as we drive. Any distraction may cause the person with ASD to lose the thread of what he is doing. For example, if my son is carrying out his morning routines and the carer arrives, he stops. Uninterrupted he will complete the steps, but once stopped he is unlikely to pick up the unfinished tasks. Task completion is important and necessary. The person offering support should wherever practicable direct the person with ASD back to the routine. This is vital if he is to have the sense of accomplishment from completing what it has been set out he will do. Presumably the routine is there for a purpose and therefore there will be consequences if it is not completed. Depending on what we were doing, finding that we have left something in the middle of it can be anything from mildly annoying (left the kitchen half cleaned) to very distressing (left the pan on the hob and burnt the house down).

Praise is important, because it promotes self-esteem. It also encourages the person to repeat the action. He can only do this if he is clear what elicited the praise, and for those with ASD this has to be absolutely explicit or he will not know. Anyone benefits from a sense of achievement. This is only gained if the task is completed and if the benefits of this completion are recognized. People need meaningful praise, and for the person with ASD this will involve making what he has achieved absolutely clear to him. For example, when he arrives at college on time, the supporter might say to him, 'Well done. You have arrived on time. There are many seats still free. You can chose where you sit. You will not miss any of the lesson today. You will be comfortable and ready for it to begin.' The supporter can reinforce how this was achieved, acknowledging the planning in looking up bus timetables, having the bus fare ready and setting the alarm clock. The regular repetition of what is gained by a particular action will, slowly but surely, establish for the person its intrinsic value.

Autistic thinking is rigid. Learning new things is a slow process, like dripping water wearing away a stone. It is easy to believe that a person with ASD never learns and that explanation is a waste of breath. This is not so. If the person offering support is prepared to repeat and reinforce, pointing out how sequences of events are linked and the results of different actions, the person supported will gradually assimilate this. People with ASD who have high intelligence learn to think their way through processes that do not come naturally. People of all intelligence are able to do this to some extent, if they are consistently and patiently explained to.

Those with ASD live in the NT world. The primary role of support must be to facilitate the understanding of it, that they need to survive.

In short:

- The person with ASD benefits from support to redirect attention to the task in hand.

- Achievement needs to be pointed out clearly, and praise given.

- Repeated explanation of cause and effect enables the person to eventually make connections himself.

Chapter 6

Communication

Difficulties

Difficulty with communication is a core problem for those with autism spectrum disorder (ASD). Some people have little or no speech, some have an extensive vocabulary, some make grammatical mistakes, some have a wide use of language – but all people with ASD have problems with communication. These problems are extremely complex, leading to much misunderstanding, confusion and stress. The more sophisticated the person's language is the greater the problem may be. Ros Blackburn, a highly intelligent British woman with ASD who gives many talks on the subject, highlights that a person's ability can also be their greatest disability. As a verbal, intellectually able woman, she finds that people do not appreciate the support that she needs in everyday and social situations. The power to have a seemingly normal conversation can cause many troubles for a person with ASD by giving a false impression of their comprehension.

My son is fine at holding a conversation, but has great difficulty communicating. His difficulties are exacerbated, because they are masked by his facility with language. As a supply teacher, I was covering a French class in a mainstream secondary school. We began with some simple conversation followed by written exercises. One pupil (who was neurotypical (NT)) held a perfect conversation, giving sensible responses to everything I said. Shortly after they began the written work, she asked for help, and I was shocked to discover that she understood virtually nothing of the excellent French conversation we had. Her replies made absolute sense. If I had been asked about her ability, I would have said she had a good grasp of the language and have had no doubt that she followed completely all that was said. It is very difficult concept to grasp that a person can have a conversation without engaging with its meaning, but many people with ASD are fascinated by patterns of language, rather than seeing it as a communication tool.

John enjoyed learning to read and mastered the skill very adequately, but he reaches the end of the passage totally unable to say what he has read. I find it perplexing that there can be any pleasure in reading without gaining information or following a story, but the act of decoding appears sufficient for him. Similarly, he may be engrossed in conversation with someone, but if he is asked about it afterwards he often has little idea of what was said. He will neither recall nor act upon what has been discussed. A graphic example of his failure to process language happened when he was packing things into the fridge a few days ago. I warned him to be careful if he stood up as I was opening the microwave on the shelf above. He looked up at me and the open door, smiled, said yes and promptly stood up, crashing into it.

People with limited language skills are often echolalic, simply repeating back what has been said. They mimic, often producing a good likeness of the person they have heard. People will pick up and repeat a phrase, perhaps a catchphrase from the TV, which they like the sound of. They also retain longer sections of speech, which can be used in dialogue. It is possible to have a conversation, which is a mechanical putting together of correct phrases, but with no deeper meaning.

Speech and manner may take on the cadences, inflections and phrasings of people the person has contact with. This causes countless misunderstandings for my son, as he will pick up on and reflect the views of the person he is talking to but may then talk to someone with a completely different view of the situation and do exactly the same.

Communication is an extremely complicated skill, with even the most intelligent, articulate people finding themselves at times unable to put across their meaning, feeling they are misunderstood and cannot explain an argument or manage to express their true feelings. We all at times misinterpret what someone means to say. Communication is at the heart of human life. It is vital to personal relationships, work skills and every aspect of daily living.

The first step in offering support has to be acknowledging the complexity of communication, and the effect of ASD on a person's ability to understand input and to express their own needs and thoughts. Much skill, thought and specialized input is needed to begin to unravel the problems.

In short:

- Those offering support need to be aware that the affects of ASD on communication are extremely complex.

- They need to be aware that the person with ASD may be following a pattern and not take the same meaning from the conversation as others do.

Clear communication

After recognizing the enormous challenge the person with ASD faces in all areas of communication, practical help measures are needed. Communication is chaotic, fast and infinitely varied. The first practical step is to remove any removable chaos.

People generally focus on people. In any space our attention is drawn to people, and if someone is talking to us we may miss other things that are happening around us. For the person with ASD everything fights for attention. It is difficult to listen if there is too much happening; too much background noise, too much visually to take in or another demand on one's interest. When speaking, the supporter needs to be aware that the person may simply be unable to take on board what is being said if he is doing something or there is too much sensory stimulation around. The implications for support are to be very aware of the environment, and, if the matter to discuss is important, remove distractions or go to a calmer place.

Anyone who needs to explain something should try to ensure that they are clear and unambiguous in what he says. This is much easier said than done! We use intonation, irony, idiom, facial expression and we make sweeping assumptions about the other person's perception of the world being the same as ours. John, struggling to carry a selection of Christmas decorations, threw them into the air when a friend directed him to juggle the load. The world would be dull if we stuck only to basic statements, but when there is particular information that it is important to give, it helps to think carefully about phrasing. Sentences are best kept short and simple, giving concrete examples.

Language disorder is part of ASD and not linked to intelligence. A person may grasp a difficult academic concept, and yet struggle with a seemingly simple instruction. Matt has no difficulty with working at degree level in his subject, but notes in his account that he requires support with interpretation of what a question requires of him. It is vital to ensure that important information is given clearly. Often it is helpful to also put it in writing for the person to refer back to and digest at leisure.

Those spending time with people with ASD realize that it is necessary to check that information has been received. Talking as parents, we found that we all knew the phenomenon of our son or daughter not registering what was said to him or her. This could be despite the child's giving an appropriate verbal response. As most people learn to automatically pick up non-verbal signals, we subconsciously recognized subtle cues to the fact our child 'had gone'. Several parents reported how they would ask directly if they had been heard, checking by asking for a repetition or questioning. It is not necessarily enough to ask the person to respond to questions about what has been said. They are likely to give a false impression of comprehension, by using the pattern of the conversation to give back what the person has imparted to them, without necessarily taking any meaning from the words. Wherever possible this should be done by giving examples and asking what the person would do in a particular situation. So, when discussing the danger of talking to strangers, instead of asking for a repetition of rules (such as only give short polite answers to someone you do not know), say you are at the bus stop and someone asks you what the time is – ask the person with ASD, 'What do you say? What do you do? What do you not say?' And so on.

Whenever a relevant situation arises in practice, it should be pointed out. If a stranger speaks to the person, it is an opportunity to analyse whether they have reacted properly. If the person with ASD spoke to someone he did not know personally, there can be discussion about whether that was appropriate. If the person offering support either speaks to or is spoken to by someone, the interaction provides a chance for learning. It is as important to pick up on a proper response as it is to warn the person if his response is not appropriate to the situation. Reassurance and praise are very necessary to someone trying to make sense of unpredictable situations. This builds his confidence and increases his ability to learn. If the person's response has been inappropriate, this needs to be pointed out with a chance for him to work out what the consequence may have been. However, it is vital to concentrate on the positive, so the person needs time to consider what it would have been better to do or say. Giving praise for this and reinforcing clearly what should have been done focuses on the learning to be gained. Where the response was correct, the person offering support can capitalize on the situation by ensuring the person supported knows why this was a good response, praising and talking through simply what has been done.

Care should be taken not to give too much information at one time. People with ASD generally process language slowly and have difficulty handling a lot of verbal input. It may be obvious that a person is struggling to cope with a conversation, because of their response. When a discussion is going well it is tempting to prolong it, but it is better to summarize progress and allow the person time to process without overloading. People with ASD work through matters slowly, and speed of discussion is problematic. John frequently makes a comment that is inexplicable at first, until I realize he is picking up on a conversation we had minutes, hours or even days ago and has needed this time lag to formulate his reaction. So time needs to be offered to assimilate information before a response is expected. A few bullet points written out can serve as a concrete reminder for the person to consider at his own pace. Once this information has been digested, understood and any points discussed, there is a firm basis to move on from.

The person offering support can assist by being alert to situations where it may be difficult to follow what is being said, or too much information is given for the person to assimilate. If, for example, it is in a meeting, he may be able to pause it to check that the person is understanding and is comfortable with the format, so that every effort is made to ensure that the communication is clear. If this is not possible the supporter can go over the main points in a more suitable environment, and at a slower pace.

In short:

- The person offering support needs to be aware of the effects of distractions on a person's ability to hear speech.

- Explanations need to be kept concise and clear.

- Understanding needs to be checked frequently.

- Those giving support can assist by taking opportunities to reinforce meaning when relevant situations arise in practice.

- A short verbal and/or written summary is useful at the end of any discussion.

- People with ASD need time to process what has been said.

Listening

Of the two sides of communication listening is the most important. Effective support can only be given after carefully listening to the needs of the person to be supported. I write about listening after talking only because it is such an immensely difficult skill to achieve.

To truly hear what another person means to communicate is the most demanding thing to do and a much underrated skill. Talking is an active role; it usually has a purpose. If we wish to put across a point, we put much thought into how we will word our explanation and reasoning. Listening may be seen as passive. A person may have to overcome nerves and be psyched up to talk, particularly if there is a large group to be addressed; whilst conversely it is possible to relax and sit back when not called on to speak. The theory is that those not speaking in a meeting are listening, but of course this is not always the case. If we are speaking we concentrate, assuming those around are listening and will notice if we make a mistake; if we are not speaking no one can tell if we are listening or mentally composing our shopping list. Even when we believe we are listening, it is all too easy to overlay what we hear with our own preconceptions. We hate it when we feel that someone has not listened to what we said, when we have been misinterpreted or our intentions misjudged; we then blame the failure on the other person's listening skills. Far more often, however, the onus for accurate communication is put on the ability of the speaker rather than the listener. People with ASD may have some difficulties with their verbal expression, but this does not mean that those around can blame them for all communication failures, only that those giving support must listen more carefully.

Many of those I know with ASD, including John, complain frequently that they are not listened to, meaning that the sense of what they intended to say has not been heard. Some are aware that they have had difficulty expressing what they would have liked to say. Often they feel they have told others their views and are very disappointed to find they have not got the point across.

Listening to their meaning is a great challenge when supporting people with ASD. My son may tell one person something, whilst telling another the complete opposite. If he feels it is going to be impossible to achieve something that he has been asking for, he will become frustrated and may appear to change his mind. Those with ASD live in the moment with a poor sense of time. Waiting is an agony. Often rather than face more disappointment at not achieving what he wants, John will reject the aim. He was keen to go to college, but after much discussion he was still not enrolled on a course. Rather than face more uncertainty, he began declaring loudly that he did not want to go. He complains that staff did not assist him to find a course, but had said several times very forcefully that he did not want to go. The result:

complete confusion. Paradoxically, when John repeats the same phrase adamantly it is sometimes what he least wants. Those giving support need to be aware of the confusion that can build up within and ripple out from the person they support. Space, understanding and specialist advice is needed.

For a person with ASD words have a literal meaning, which is often demonstrated by their failure to understand idioms or figurative use of language. As an able university student, Matt describes his taking things people say literally as a cause of misunderstandings. Some of our sayings are bizarre if taken literally, but the NT mind rarely registers this, moving instantaneously on to the meaning. We also register implications and read more into words than is said. One of my daughters, as a young child, said to me, 'I will never leave home, Mummy.' I took this as a compliment to me and my care. My ego came crashing down when, in response to my enquiring why, she replied factually, 'Because I cannot reach to open the door.'

People with ASD often mean what they say and nothing more. For people generally what they say is tempered by the effect it will have on others, and they read this expectation into what they hear. For example, if I did not like a person's dress sense, I would not tell them every time I saw them that I disliked their clothes. If I did they would quickly take a dislike to me and assume I did not like them. We would both interpret repeated criticism of what the person wore as unfriendly. A person with ASD might be immediately struck by the person's clothes and regularly comment on these whenever they met. The statement will simply be his spontaneous response to the clothes and have no bearing on how he feels about the person; however, few NTs would see it that way. I hope this illustrates how very easy it is to place totally the wrong construction on intentions of a person with ASD. It is difficult to remain objective and not add our own layers of meaning.

As I have become more adept at picking up my son's meanings, different problems emerge for me. It is particularly frustrating when he realizes that he has somehow been misunderstood and asks me to help him to get his meaning across. When I do so I may appear to contradict him as he continues to act and talk in the way that originally misled people. Aaargh! As a professional counsellor, I know that it is often easier to confide in a stranger than to talk to your nearest and dearest. People communicate information that they would find difficult to tell, parents, children or partners for fear of the effect it would have. However, this is not necessarily so if you have ASD. The familiar is more comfortable and the person is likely to feel more confident talking to someone who is used to his way of communication. The implications are for the professional support worker to bear in mind that usual suppositions do not necessarily apply. People with ASD may talk freely to parents about a situation that most would not discuss.

It is often said that people with ASD do not lie. This idea appears rooted in the fact that they can be brutally honest at times, due to a lack of recognition of social cues and of awareness as to when it is tactful to remain silent. John sat in his dear grandmother's living room and happily announced that he would never paint his house that colour. A conscientious, intelligent woman, describing how she had been unable to hold down work, related an incident where a person was asking to see one of the managers. The manager's secretary, having been warned he did not want to see this person, told her that he would not be in until later. My friend thought she was being helpful in intervening to insist that this was wrong as she had just seen him – until that is she was invited into the manager's office to discuss this.

This lack of guile has led to the notion that those with ASD always tell the truth. This is obviously not so when we consider their chameleon-like tendency to fit in with the speech patterns of those around. A major factor too is the person's jumbled view of the world. People with ASD often confabulate, that is they make things up to fill in the gaps. Some people on the autism spectrum appear to have no interest in others. Most of those I know are anxious to please, to fit in and be liked. Tragically they simply lack many of the social skills that facilitate this. Attempts to say the 'right thing' may cause more trouble. Their efforts to converse sometimes result in stories that are so incredible that they are easily recognized as fantasy; others are plausible and so the person listening responds and the conversation continues in the same vein. Either way the outcome is not good once it is obvious that the person is not telling the truth. The careers advisor interviewing John had no reason to doubt his answers, until he told him about his experience of playing football for Manchester United. The advisor was outraged, feeling his time was wasted and that John was lying to him. We naturally assign motive to the behaviour, assuming the person has deliberately set out to mislead us, whereas the teller is probably simply lost in the role oblivious to the reaction of the listener.

As the person giving support it is important to unravel from the confusion, what the person truly wishes to communicate. In all the complexity of this issue, the best place to start is as always with the basics. It is essential to have a quiet place with as few distractions as possible. When faced with a meeting with his social worker that he considered very important, John dressed in his suit and planned to sit at the dining table. His social worker had also given thought to the situation. His plan was to talk whilst they walked or sat in the park, as he felt this would create an informal neutral environment where John would feel relaxed about talking. This reasoning would probably hold true for most young men, but people with ASD tend to prefer formal to informal, the familiar to the unfamiliar, and certainly when faced with such a challenging task as talking, want an environment where there are no activities and sensations to tug at their attention. The person with ASD needs plenty of time to formulate what he wants to say. The listener may be uncomfortable if there is a silence, but the person struggling for words will be focusing on his thoughts and it is vital to wait.

If the person is giving out contradictory information or appears to be confabulating, the best approach may be the straightforward one, of explaining the reason for asking. The principle applies that the person may need to have the implicit made explicit. The careers advisor knows that he is asking about the applicant's work experience to assess what he can do and what work would be suitable. Explaining in simple terms exactly what type of information is needed and why gives the clarity to focus John's mind on what is required of him in the situation.

For most people with ASD, it is easier to talk if there are fewer people in the group. In a large meeting there is too much to take in, and few silences in which to process what has been said. Unfortunately the professional response to any major matter is to call a meeting so that all parties can put forward their views. John does not like meetings of more than three or four selected people. He dutifully struggles to give the 'right' answers. There is often a written sheet he can study for clues; some subjects are so familiar that he knows the required response; if he is stuck someone will kindly help him by giving prompts. John is easily led; he picks up a clue and gives a response. A person offering support may wittingly or unwittingly lead him towards what they consider the best solution. This is accepted, often passed on, perhaps acted on and he is prompted to the same response in future. So we often hurtle on unstoppably in a direction that causes him ever-increasing stress, with all around believing they are supporting his desires. Perhaps a better approach would be to allow the person to express his view to his facilitator and make an audio or video recording to present to a meeting when it is necessary for several people to be involved.

People with ASD benefit from access to a person who is a trained psychologist or counsellor with experience of the disorder to aid them with communication. We would consider it unthinkable to conduct an interview with a deaf person without an appropriate interpreter. ASD causes severe problems with communication, but, because of the hidden nature of the disability, people do not receive support which is afforded automatically to those with more easily measurable disabilities.

In short:

- Those offering support need to be aware of the effects of distractions on a person's ability to formulate what he wants to say.

- Important matters should be discussed in a familiar environment with the minimum of extraneous stimulus.

- The person must be allowed plenty of time (and some more) to work out what he needs to say.

- Beware of reading more into words than is said.

- People with ASD should have access to a specialist psychologist or counsellor who can support their communication.

Case study 6.1: Harry

Harry's account below highlights vividly the difficulties he has with communication. It demonstrates the deep frustration that he feels when unable to communicate as he would wish. It shows the dangers inherent in making mistakes in non-verbal communications, and illustrates the stress this places on Harry and his family. Harry's support profile can be found in Appendix 2.

Harry *Harry has been in his current job in transport for 30 years. He has two adult children, one of whom lives with him.*

Harry vividly remembers being struck by a ball in the playground when he was five years old. The teacher demanded why he was crying, but he was totally unable to tell her. The words would not form in his head and he was chastised for crying for no reason. Other children ran around saying, 'What is your name?', but Harry did not know how to reply and they grew impatient with him.

Unusually for children in the 1950s, Harry was assessed and ASD was recognized at this early stage. He was fortunate in having supportive parents who challenged the first doctor's recommendation that he should be sent away from home. They sought a second opinion from a doctor in London, who gave them good advice on how to support Harry. The primary school were progressive and accepting of him and his difficulties. Harry particularly enjoyed maths.

When Harry was aged 11, there were fears that he would not manage in the large classes at the secondary modern school. Instead he went to boarding school for what he now recalls as the worst five years of his life. He did not like being away from home, found it hard to make friends and was bullied. He was afraid of heights and froze in panic when climbing the ladders in the gym.

Returning home, Harry had lost touch with friends from primary school. However, he went to the local college and gained another five O Levels, in English, sciences and geology. He enjoyed his studies, but found exams difficult. He saw so many possible ways of answering the questions, that he was never sure what was required. He enjoyed Friday nights at the pub and was generally accepted into the group. He realizes though that some people were teasing and taking advantage of him.

A series of jobs followed. Harry is still upset as he remembers how the boss of the farm labourers, shouted at him, saying that at 20 he was still acting like a little boy. He travelled to Scotland in the hope of better work prospects, but was unable to keep a job for long. One lasted only two days before the manager let him go, saying that people did not like working with him. Harry is a conscientious worker, who has held his current job for 30 years, but he still finds that he is sometimes in trouble for things he does not understand or that appear trivial to him.

After a two-year courtship, Harry was married for 20 years and had two daughters. He feels that his ASD played a part in the break-up of his marriage. Harry is a friendly man who likes to socialize, but he tends to stay home most nights and keeps himself to himself. This is provoked by anxiety that he may say or do the wrong thing. He recalls instances of chatting to people in pubs, but being told abruptly that he was interrupting a private conversation.

Harry is obviously fond of his mother and kindly clears away the crockery for her as we leave. He speaks affectionately of his father, who died 15 years previously and whom he describes as his dear friend. As his mother and I talk, we realize he is no longer following the conversation but is still focused on a subject important to him. He does not respond to what we ask, but returns to his preferred subject. We both know that this is simply the way it is with ASD. Harry is aware that he misses social cues. His children have pointed out to him instances when he stands too close to someone and infringes on their personal space. As he idly watched a man who reminded him of an acquaintance, his daughter warned him that he was staring. His mother describes how he continued to chat to two women who obviously did not want his attention. Harry asks her what the signs were that he missed; but she is at a loss to explain the subtle body language used. He is a gentle man, who is upset that his actions may have troubled anyone. He tells me sadly about talking to some women at work. He thought he was being friendly and getting on with them, but the boss warned him he frightened them.

Harry is fortunate in having a supportive family. It is, however, stressful worrying that he might unintentionally offend someone. He enjoys attending the Tuesday Club, as he can relax knowing his ASD is understood, and he is accepted for himself.

More than words

Most of us can tell when a friend is upset as soon as we see his face or hear his voice. Ask us how we knew and we would have to think long and hard to work out the clues. In an instant, we will have unthinkingly picked up and interpreted a mass of subtle signals: facial expression, posture, tone of voice. It is an important skill that most people develop naturally, but this does not happen for those with ASD. They do not receive much non-verbal information, or send it and may be seen as poker-faced: Matt described in Case study 2.1 how shocked he was at his 'miserable' expression on the school photo. There are educational materials aimed at teaching facial expressions by using actors to demonstrate the various emotions. In practice the difference between expressions can be very subtle, and they may change rapidly. As a member of the social club asked me for advice on how he could read faces, I was aware of my expression flickering between puzzlement, a (I hope) reassuring smile and concentration in seconds. Harry's mother was equally at a loss when he asked her what the signs were that she picked up and he did not which would have indicated his attentions were unwelcome.

People with ASD do not give the responses which are automatic to most people, or recognize unwritten rules that govern social interaction. Like many with ASD, John does not make good eye contact and may stand too close to another person. Interpretation and use of such things are so woven into our daily lives, it is impossible to realize how intricate, how essential they are, until we see someone who has not developed these. The supporter needs to be aware of when such behaviour becomes problematic. The simple act of standing too close to another person affects the relationship, making them feel uncomfortable or possibly threatened. This is certainly the case with John, because of his size. Harry's family have pointed out to him instances where he has done this. However, he is aware that he does not read the situation for himself and anxious that he may cause offence.

We encouraged John to look at the distance others kept. Standing close to him did not worry him and so we had to explain how others might feel. We then had a simple hand signal as a prompt to move if he was encroaching on someone else's space. Being aware of and assisting with noticeable social gaffes can avert awkward situations. As we add layers of meaning to innocent remarks, so we also read far more into non-verbal forms of communication than may be intended. For their own safety, people may need to learn the effect of behaviours, such as watching someone too intently, and be given support to modify their behaviour. An ongoing programme can build a repertoire of non-verbal behaviour to avert some difficulties.

Many do not understand the reciprocity fundamental to conversation. If the conversation is not about a subject of immediate interest to him the person with ASD may say nothing, look bored or even walk away. On the other hand, he is the ultimate 'anorak', droning on endlessly about a subject that may hold no interest for the listener. He will not recognize subtle (or even obvious) hints that he is boring the other person. John's subject is popular music; for his friend Tim it is trains; a young woman I know admits candidly that her favourite topic is herself. My mother's response when John is engrossed in a monologue is straightforward, simple and the most effective I have heard. She says, 'I know nothing about modern music and have no interest in CDs, so we will have to talk about something else.' This does not stop John returning to the subject, but it stops him immediately and, after many repetitions, he does occasionally remember that this is not a topic to talk to her about. As with any learning, the key is a clear explanation repeated regularly.

Conversation is a necessary attainment to some extent in all walks of life. The skills involved are so intricate and multifarious that it would be impossible to instruct anyone fluently in the art. People with ASD are often saddened that they are not included in social groups and totally unable to explain why. A student agreed to accompany a friend, who has ASD, to the union bar in an attempt to (in his words) tell him what he was doing wrong. The friend with ASD gallantly offered to buy the drinks, before ploughing his way to the bar and demanding them from the barman who was part way through an order. He planted the drinks on the table of two fellow students, and launched into conversation. Support with some basic rules, such as learning to wait your turn at the bar, greeting acquaintances, asking if you may join them and not interrupting can go some way to helping. Such small differences add up to others receiving a more positive perception of the person.

Part of the difficulty with two-way conversation is the speed of processing required, which is an overwhelming problem for most people with ASD in a group. With people chipping in different comments, perhaps throwing in jokes and innuendos, they are likely to be at a loss. They almost always prefer one to one conversation to group discussion, and small intimate gatherings to parties. The supporter can try to assist the person with ASD to select social venues where he will be more comfortable.

Individuals have different needs. Some people with ASD have little desire for social contact, and conversation skills are mainly for necessary functional communication. Others seek companionship, friendship and/or a partner. As with all aspects of support the priorities and needs will have to be worked out with the individual.

The last word on conversation has to go to a friend who frankly said, 'I know I am supposed to ask about other people. My parents have taught me how to have a conversation – but really all I want to do is talk about myself.'

In short:

- Non-verbal communication skills do not develop naturally for people with ASD.

- Those offering support can assist by identifying behaviours that may cause problems.

- Despite the complexity, some behaviours can be explained and taught.

- Steady teaching of simple rules can ease some situations.

In all its complexity

We all communicate from our own frame of reference. How we react to and understand what is said to us depends upon our life experiences and our personality. People are generally drawn to those with similar backgrounds. Take a group of friends and they are likely in the main to be in the same age group, probably similar professional and educational experiences and lifestyle. We communicate more easily with those who have much in common with us. When we consider this it follows that as people with ASD have such markedly different perceptions, there are enormous problems to overcome.

The person with ASD misses or places an atypical interpretation on much that is said. Various aspects of the disorder, paradoxes and contradictions, confabulations and mimicking, combine to make it difficult for others to unravel what the person may truly want to communicate. This is the source of many difficulties and misunderstandings. It is an area where a great deal of research is needed, and specialist support is vital.

CHAPTER 7

Social Interaction

Difference

Life cannot be compartmentalized. It would perhaps be more understandable to those with autism spectrum disorder (ASD) if it could. Communication difficulties obviously cause enormous problems in social situations. It is less apparent, but organization also has a great bearing on these. How to invite a friend to go on an outing is not necessarily the only problem, there is also where to go, when to go and how to get there. There are numerous details that most people would find incidental, but which can appear monumental to someone with ASD. Any social interaction requires a multiplicity of skills, which most employ with little conscious thought. Many are so automatic and subtle that it is difficult to put your finger on what is missing when social behaviour is not quite right.

People with ASD often appear aloof and uninterested. John often focuses an object which for us is an unimportant part of the background. With a lack of empathy and the tendency to say whatever they think, it is not surprising that people with ASD often do not project a good image of themselves. There is a whole stratum of social behaviour that is missing. Very able people who want to be on good terms with colleagues and to have friends find themselves shunned, even bullied, with no idea where they have gone wrong. A young man could not understand why the girl he had known, been keen on for a while and finally asked out, suddenly walked away as they arranged the date. I do not know exactly what happened, but I suspect she was not impressed that, as he entered the details in his diary, he asked her what her name was.

People with ASD do not know how to play the social games, and this frequently makes them appear rude and self-centred. In conversation John launches straight into what he wants to say, talking at people with little apparent interest in them. If he, or one of his friends, becomes bored at a social gathering and would rather be at home pursuing his interests, he is likely to say so. If someone says something that John does not want to hear he simply ignores them, and carries on as if they have not spoken. Harry (see Case study 6.1) switches off from the conversation between his mother, himself and me, when it moves from the topic of most interest to him. These type of traits do not make people with ASD immediately attractive and often lead to isolation and loneliness.

Some people with ASD appear content with a solitary life, with leisure time centred on interests rather than relationships. However, many people with ASD do want a social life, companionship and a partner and may identify this as an area where they need support. Their attempts to do the 'right thing' to establish a friendship may again be inappropriate. A major stumbling block is in recognizing social boundaries. A person with ASD will not pick up social cues to tell if his attention is welcome or not. If he is accepted into the conversation in a public place, he may not understand that this does not put him on the same footing as others in the group who may have known each other for a number of years. Harry's experiences in the pub were most likely caused by people responding his remarks on the level of a polite response to a casual stranger, but not expecting to engage any further. A person with ASD will not interpret the subtle differences between dealings with a sociable stranger and a friend, between a person who is a work colleague and a social acquaintance, between a friend of the opposite sex and a potential partner.

We all make blunders in relationships. We misjudge what is acceptable in a situation, mistake another person's intention or misinterpret someone's meaning. We then feel upset, isolated and embarrassed. People with ASD are more prone to doing this sort of thing than most – and they do experience the same unpleasant aftermath. I have heard others say, even thought it myself, that at least the person will have been unaware of how others feel about him. After years of experience I know this is not so, but is one of the great myths about autism. Many factors contribute to this impression. People are apt not to show subtleties of feeling in their expression or tone of voice. They have great trouble expressing themselves in any circumstance, and an emotional one is the hardest of all. They may be silent and stony-faced at times of great emotion and so give the impression of indifference and heartlessness. Confusion and slowness of processing are major contributors to this notion. People with ASD describe being 'overloaded' at times of great emotions. From the descriptions some have given me it sounds as if, rather than being insensitive, they are so hypersensitive when emotion is intense that they shut down as a coping mechanism.

People with ASD, however, do not take in all the nuances and shades of a social exchange. They may stumble on repeating mistakes, oblivious that anything is wrong. My son is one of the many I know who would regularly happily join a lively, laughing group, only to suddenly realize that he was in fact the butt of the joke. It is only much later that the realization comes to them of the real meaning and implications of an event or conversation. In common with many with ASD, Mark, Harry, Matt and Darren featured in the case studies all report similar scenarios.

I have spoken to many who have been very hurt that a friendship has failed, or that they have been unable to relate to colleagues, but they will be unable to understand why. It is possible that hours, days, weeks later they may realize where they went wrong, but by then everyone else has moved on and the situation is beyond rescue. Sometimes other people become so annoyed that they explain very abruptly. A friend's work colleague angrily told her in detail how she spoke about herself too much, did not listen to others and was selfish and rude. This took her some time to work through; she had had no idea of the impact of her behaviour. Years later she was still very upset that she had offended her workmates, and yet I suspect they were totally unaware of her feelings.

No one can exist totally isolated from society, and at a basic level some with ASD will need support to enable them to interact without being taken advantage of by, or causing offence to, members of the public and/or colleagues. Other children in school found it amusing to ask John to do things they would not do themselves. He would be happy to join in thinking they were friendly, only to be teased or told off. He never picked up the cues quickly enough to run or cover what he was doing, and so took the blame not only for what he did, but often I suspect also for others. This is a story I have heard from numerous people with ASD. Adults with ASD are equally vulnerable to being misled with unpleasant consequences for them. They are also at risk from a naive remark, or looking too long and curiously at strangers, which can land someone in a great deal of trouble. So anyone offering support can assist by being alert to such situations and taking steps to support the person when he may endanger himself.

The lack of social understanding is fundamental to the condition. No treatment, training or therapy will make it go away. Support can provide the person with coping strategies, but it is vital never to forget that they are only crutches; the disability has not ceased to exist. The underlying difficulties are still there, and in fact the person may be working very hard to maintain what appears as a normal level of functioning. Coping well is a double-edged sword; the better a person manages, the more likely he is to be judged harshly when he does make a mistake.

It is my experience that far from being unfeeling, people with ASD are often very sensitive. They care deeply about those close to them and are unfailingly loyal. They are hurt by rejection, lack of understanding and bullying. There is often no one they can turn to for support. As Matt (Case study 2.1) says, simply having someone to talk things through with is a great help.

The person offering support has to be willing to make the quantum leap from our neurotypical (NT) world into an understanding of how it is for someone with ASD. There is a need to put aside judgements based on an inappropriate social interaction and see the whole person. Lack of social skills does not equal lack of feeling. Listening to the person carefully can tease out their perspective. Ideally the person supporting will be willing to stand in the person's corner and advocate for him.

In short:

- People with ASD do want relationships.

- Assistance with social relationships may be a reason for requesting support.

- The disability masks the person's true feelings and leads to misunderstanding.

- The person offering support needs to ensure the individual is not endangered by social ineptitude.

- Social impairment is fundamental to ASD and cannot be 'cured'.

Coping strategies

Some people with ASD are able to think their way through social situations. They teach themselves or have been taught to interpret non-verbal signals. They can use cognition to remember that the other person may feel differently to them, and to compute what their perception and emotions may be.

This is a slow, cumbersome method compared to the automatic, rapid assimilation that those without ASD make. Even those who compensate well appear slow, stilted, awkward, and are liable to make significant mistakes. A few find a lifestyle and strategies that enables them to manage comfortably with no more problems in this area than your average NT.

Social rules can make a person and their behaviour more acceptable. Simple matters, like saying 'Hello' and asking how a person is make a difference to how someone is perceived. People with ASD tend to be focused on a purpose and social niceties do not come to mind. If they are approaching the person to ask them something, or for something, they will steam straight in and make their demand. This single-mindedness naturally comes across as rudeness. I have known a student, intent on asking something of his tutor, to simply find where she was teaching, walk into the lecture and interrupt her mid-flow with his query. The supporter can assist a person to recognizing the impact of behaviours, such as waiting until someone has finished speaking or concentrating on a task before talking, and offering encouragement in practising these.

Realizing the two-way nature of conversation is not easy. At the most basic level, there is a need to learn to take turns; to talk, but also to allow the other person to talk. Then there is the requirement to show interest in the other person. Even with my intimate knowledge of his disabilities at times I feel hurt by John's apparent indifference. It would be nice when I came back from holiday to be asked if I enjoyed myself, rather than be met with a catalogue of problems he had in my absence. The person offering support can assist by giving reminders about life events for others, and prompts about apposite comments and queries relating to these.

Many people will want to expand their social circles. A good starting point is to look at interests and find activities related to these. Libraries and leisure centres have details of evening classes, sports activities and local interest groups. Various social venues may be uncomfortable, because of noise levels, general excess of sensory input, numbers of people and speed of interactions. A stable group that meets at a regular time for a set purpose – such as an art group, badminton club or cookery class – is likely to be more accessible. A shared interest or activity provides a natural topic of conversation, and so can overcome some difficulties involved in relating to others and making small talk. Possible topics of conversation can be discussed beforehand and, if the person offering support is on hand, he can help by offering prompts.

I have joined a group made up of people with ASD, friends, families and professionals who organize a social club locally. There are regular evening meetings at a venue that has facilities for some games, craft activities, music and refreshments. It is a great success. It is well attended and people enjoy themselves. A comment often made by the users, who have ASD, is that it is a safe environment where they can relax. Many have experience of being teased and know that this is a place where their differences are accepted. There is no fear of being caught out or taken advantage of. As with any group, people with ASD appreciate the opportunity to meet others who share some similar experiences to their own. They are able to support each other by talking though events and exchanging ideas. The wider aim is that, apart from the club nights, it provides an opportunity for people to establish friendships and meet up outside this venue. It develops confidence and social skills, that can be reinforced in other situations.

The social arena is certainly a complex area of support as no two situations are ever the same and there is a multiplicity of variables, which must all be handled simultaneously. What is correct behaviour in one setting is totally unacceptable in another. Behaviour that is fine in the pub on Saturday night is definitely not in the office on Monday. The same action that elicits praise in one set of circumstances may be unacceptable in another.

John knows I appreciate it when he does jobs around the house, especially heavy ones. On Wednesday night he puts the dustbin out to be emptied, and one week he thought he would help a few other people by doing theirs for them. To his mind this is a kind, praiseworthy thing to do and he is thanked for it. It did not occur to him that others would be very concerned to see a stranger come into their garden after dark. If they challenged him, they would be unlikely to believe his explanation that he was trying to be helpful by putting their dustbin out. It is easy to see how such a simple situation could escalate. It is confusing for those with ASD when the world is so inconsistent and illogical, and their well-meaning gestures are liable to be misinterpreted. It is easy for the person offering support to fall into the trap of misunderstanding the person they work with. It is one thing reading the words in a book and having a concept of how ASD affects a person; it is quite another to hold that in mind when the person you are supporting does something that appears rude, unfeeling or bizarre. The person giving support, informally or formally, would benefit greatly from having regular contact with a professional with whom they can discuss concerns.

Like many John cannot understand the concept of distance. This is true physically in that he may stand uncomfortably close, or wander into someone's private space, but also in that he does not appreciate that there is a difference in how you relate to people depending on how familiar they are. Those giving support can explain and teach about physical closeness and private spaces, but closeness in relationships is more complicated. Youngsters with ASD given a set of concentric circles and asked to put those closest to them in the centre working outwards, generally organize this on a geographical basis. John had in the central circle people he had barely spoken to as they lived in the same street, whilst his grandparents were in the outer circle as they lived some distance away. This is a graphic demonstration of the deficit in social awareness. Typically people with ASD do not realize that the way you speak and relate to one person will be very different from the way you should speak and relate to another. This is an area where a great deal of support is needed to avoid misunderstandings. Jovial banter heard amongst friends is probably not the thing to say to your boss, nor do you tell intimate details to a stranger at the bus stop who comments on the weather. Professional support staff should ensure that they maintain a professional distance. It is easy when someone has many hours of support to slip into a more familiar attitude. This may be more comfortable for the supporter but it sends out mixed messages, and those with ASD do not cope with this.

But then of course relationships change and evolve. Every friend was a stranger at sometime, and a boy/girlfriend may decide they would rather revert to that state.

Rules are a blunt instrument to tackle such delicate problems but can be of use, particularly with casual exchanges, such as in shops. Subtleties are always the missing element. Enquiring about someone's health/well-being is polite; asking too many questions is intrusive. Finding that fine line is difficult for all; impossible for someone with ASD. My son certainly tries to learn social etiquette. Describing a visit to one of his support worker's houses, he said it smelt of cigarettes and was dirty and untidy, 'But,' he finished triumphantly, 'I said it was very nice.'

As a complete programme, the person with ASD needs ongoing discussion with a psychologist or counsellor with experience of ASD. Feedback is needed from those offering support to raise any concerns no matter how trivial they may appear. A programme of support can then be devised and monitored by the specialist.

In short:

- The person offering support should be vigilant and aware of potential difficulties in social situations.

- Some social rules can be taught.

- A person with ASD is likely to enjoy pastimes that involve an activity rather than simply chat.

- Most people like to spend time with their own peer group; this also applies to those with ASD.

- The person giving support may need to interpret the situation for the individual.

- The key to support in social matters is a psychologist or counsellor with experience of ASD who liaises regularly with the person and those who support him.

Sex

Sex is a source of pleasure, but also of frustration and worries. Adolescents have to come to terms with many changes, and the transition from childhood to adulthood is in many ways the most difficult stage in a person's life. Finding a boyfriend or girlfriend is high on the agenda. Emotions run high; uncertainties, misunderstandings and upsets are rife. Given the general social difficulties of the person with ASD, the problems are exacerbated for them. If a person of the opposite sex is friendly, it is difficult to interpret whether they wish to continue a friendship, or whether there is potential to develop the relationship. NTs agonize over this type of predicament, and so it is easy to see how the situation will be severely problematic for the person with ASD. This may be a situation where, even a person who generally manages with no professional support, will benefit from support from a psychologist or counsellor who has experience of working with those with ASD.

Despite all the complexities an intimate relationship is high on the agenda for most people, and this applies equally for those with ASD. Relationship counselling is usually only offered to people when it hits problems. For those with ASD it may be useful to embark on this at an earlier stage; possibly even at the point where the individual is only contemplating the desire for a boyfriend/girlfriend/partner. Current thinking is that this is a useful course of action for NTs, so that, for example, education is undertaken about relationships in school, and couples contemplating marriage are counselled. Those with ASD would benefit from being offered access to counselling from a specialist at any point.

Giving support to a person as they establish a relationship is a delicate matter. The helper has to tread the line between giving necessary support and allowing the individual and partner privacy. When a person is hoping to meet a partner, the first consideration has to be safety. The person must be aware of the dangers associated with various venues. Social conventions have become relaxed over the years, but for the person with ASD as with other areas it is beneficial to discuss and establish personal rules. These will be individual. Practical strategies can be simple, but effective. For example, ensure a taxi home is booked, that it is a familiar company or clearly marked and that it is not shared with anyone. Other matters are more complex, such as what do you do if you do not want to speak to someone who approaches you, when should you say no and how do you do this; how you approach a person you would like to talk to, how you know if they like you. There are countless variables, but some core elements can be drawn out and having a repertoire of rehearsed responses is useful. Role play is useful to consider scenarios, but the person giving support needs to remain aware of the difficulties with relating the skills to an actual situation and transferring them. What is clear in a non-pressurized, controlled, focused activity may not be easily drawn upon in actuality. As a back-up, the person should have a friend or support worker in the background, or at least have a mobile phone and someone on stand-by ready to answer it.

Problems with a new relationship are first that it is new and any change is difficult; second that it will not be static, but will evolve and alter. We try to explain to John the process of getting to know someone and have established a rough pattern to work to. Like many with ASD, he is keen to have certainties. As soon as he sees a girl as a potential girlfriend, he wants to give her this label and have this as an established, immutable fact. John needs constant reminders, not only that the girl may not wish to continue with the relationship or may prefer to be a friend, but also that he should consider whether he wants to take the relationship further. It is extremely difficult for someone with ASD to grasp that the other person may not share their view of the type of relationship, or that even if they agree to a boyfriend/girlfriend relationship, they may change their minds. People with ASD pursue a goal relentlessly and may need it reiterated many times that a relationship involves consideration of the other person's desires, as well as reviewing as it develops whether it is still right for themselves. Those offering support can only be on hand to offer guidance, and close supervision from the specialist is desirable.

Courtship is a complex social ritual. Russell Crowe, portraying the mathematician John Forbes Nash, in the film *A Beautiful Mind*, is encouraged by his fellow students to approach a girl at a bar. In response to his uncertainty, she suggests he might like to buy her a drink. He candidly replies that he is uncertain what to say, but as it is essentially about an exchange of fluids, could they go straight to the sex. He is rewarded by a slap round the face, but the cinema audience erupts into laughter. We laugh because he is expressing what many a man probably has on his mind as he approaches a female, but he will put this aside and go through the social conventions.

There are many contradictions in sexual mores. Explicit sexual scenes are acted out on mainstream television programmes, and yet less intimate sexual acts are unacceptable in public. As with any other social interaction, there are an infinite number of different behaviours, which are appropriate in differing circumstances. Crude language and jokes may be acceptable with peers in the pub or playground, but a totally different vocabulary is needed in a biology lesson. Embracing, kissing and a degree of intimacy may be permissible in a night club, but not in a well-lit restaurant and certainly not at work or during lectures. For some it will be a great challenge to assimlate the contradictory concept that, although sexual activity alone or amongst consenting adults is a natural part of life and enjoyable, it is not spoken about openly and should be enjoyed in private.

Most people want a partner to share their life and of course to enjoy a sexual relationship with. Sexual relationships are the most intimate and therefore trickiest of all to manage. Liberal attitudes to sex do not improve the situation for those with ASD. Sexual images are all around in the media; clothing may be scanty and suggestive; young people chat openly about sex – and yet there are lines which must not be crossed. Life would have been simpler when there were explicit rules, when there was less freedom and sex was for married couples. Boundaries have become blurred, and reliance has to placed on judgements of the individual situation.

Most modern rape cases are not attacks by strangers, but centre around disputes about whether consent has been given. This is not necessarily clear to an NT. If the woman is drunk does she consent? If she says no but does nothing to stop the man, does she consent? Consent is a problematic issue. Where there are likely to be difficulties, the person offering support can only try to ensure that the individual does not put himself in a situation, where there is likely to be sexual activity unless he is sure that this is what he and his partner want. A woman may be incapable of formulating and communicating her unwillingness to her partner. A man is at risk from the legal ruling that a woman may say no at any time. It may be hard enough for any to stop once a certain point is reached, but for someone with ASD it is highly unlikely that he would have the ability to process this information quickly enough to act on it.

Women with ASD are obviously at risk, as they will be unable to read the intentions behind a string of actions, or to pick up subtle sexual remarks or innuendo. They are likely to unwittingly put themselves in dangerous circumstances, or simply to be led into a situation with no understanding of the implications. When John was younger I had sympathized with my friends as they worried about the vulnerability of their pretty, disabled teenage daughter, and felt relieved that our disabled child was male. I am no longer as naive and realize that it is equally fraught for the male. Men with ASD are as innocent and susceptible to unwanted sexual approaches from both men and women as women are.

Lack of recognition of social boundaries has serious consequences when sexual behaviour is involved. A woman who makes an inappropriate sexual comment or behaves inappropriately in public, may put herself directly at risk from those who will take advantage of her naivety. The main danger to men tends to be having their behaviour misinterpreted as perverse or aggressive. A man lays himself open to arrest for indecency or even sexual assault. Careful vigilance is necessary to identify situations where people are liable to be particularly at risk, such as swimming pools and night clubs. The risks should be reiterated beforehand, and proper behaviour reinforced. However, it must be remembered that other factors, such as stress and sensory overload, may interfere with ability to recall and utilize information understood in theory.

The person with ASD is particularly at risk if he is prone to sink into fantasy and lose normal inhibitions. The dangers to such a person of sexual fantasy in a public place are obvious. No matter how remote the risk, the consequences can be so severe that it is imperative that the supporter is vigilant.

Those offering support need an understanding of the nature of ASD and the ability to appreciate that inappropriate sexual behaviour arises from lack of social skills rather than deviancy, and certainly not from maliciousness. It is vital, however, to ensure that they do not ignore any such behaviour. Supporters do not always think through the consequences for a person with ASD. We laugh when a child makes an inappropriate sexual comment, because we know that it is made innocently, without knowledge of social constraints. Those with ASD can be equally guileless. Ann Palmer (Morrell and Palmer 2006) writing about supporting her son to prepare for university, tells of discussing possible leisure pursuits, when he calmly suggested, 'And if I have a girlfriend, we can have sex during our free time' (p.127).

People often make comments that are amusing, because they are usually true and made in all innocence. I have known able, well-meaning support workers to allow a student to put their arms around them or to laugh at an inappropriate sexual comment. Staff accept this with good humour as part of the ASD, but for their own safety the person needs to be warned that sexual remarks and touching are not for general public consumption. It is one of the cases when the intricacies of what it is acceptable to say and do in different circumstances is so boggling, that the best course of action is to take as a simple guideline, that sexual remarks and physical contact should be avoided in any public place.

People with ASD can and do have successful relationships with a partner. As with any relationship, once established the person with ASD is likely to prove committed and caring.

In short:

- The difficulties that NTs have with relationships are exacerbated for those with ASD.

- People with ASD are vulnerable.

- Those offering support need to be aware of high-risk areas.

- It is safest to teach that any sexual comments and physical contact must be in private.

- Strategies are needed to ensure safety.

- Scenarios can be discussed and rehearsed.

- Close but sensitive support may be needed whilst developing a relationship.

Anti-social behaviour

ASD is a condition that affects social skills, and therefore it could be argued that 'anti-social behaviour' is inherent to the condition. However, this term covers an extremely wide range of behaviour. We may describe a person as anti-social for refusing invitations or for sitting quietly in the corner at a social gathering. A personal preference for nights in or enjoying pursuits other than parties is obviously no cause for concern. At the other end of the spectrum, there is behaviour that contravenes the law. In the UK, a child of ten who was reported to have AS was made the subject of an Anti-Social Behaviour Order under the Anti-Social Behaviour Bill (2003). The point where anti-social behaviour becomes problematic is not clear as it is dependent on subjective judgement and different situations require different behaviours.

Adequate, well-managed support addresses areas where difficulties might arise. The first step is to identify with the person, where and when he may be at risk. These may be instances where the sensory input will be too great. Overload can provoke a stress reaction, leading to behaviour which could be anti-social. John enjoys music, as do many of his friends. Much as the notion of clubbing appeals, he and his friends with ASD cannot cope with the additional sounds of chatter and glasses clattering, as well as flashing lights, smells of smoke, sweat and perfume and jostling bodies in clubs frequented by many young people. Instead he may go to a bar where he can arrive early and find a seat in an area which will be less crowded. A friend of his loves football, but hates crowds. He follows his interest by watching it on TV and through contact with the supporter's club.

Venues such as night clubs and football matches may be unsuitable because of the behaviour of others. Loud, aggressive and drunken behaviour can be frightening and provoke an odd or excessive reaction. Conversely the person may be tempted and encouraged to join in. Alcohol lowers inhibitions and leads to inappropriate actions from NTs, so its effects will involve extra risk for a person with ASD. Thorough work at the planning stage will aim to avoid high-risk situations, by finding alternatives or setting limits.

Not all potential risk situations are avoidable. Some people are at risk in a wide range of circumstances, and for some any contact with members of the public could be problematic. Clear discussion and having strategies planned in advance are effective tools. These ensure that reminders of correct behaviour are given before approaching a situation where difficulties could occur. Any indication that the behaviour is likely to occur should result in a discreet warning, possibly through a pre-arranged signal. Social behaviour does not develop spontaneously in a person with ASD, and he will need clear, direct instruction.

People with ASD learn behaviours slowly. It is important for anyone offering support to recognize how difficult this is for them, or the task of supporting with behaviour will be frustrating and it may appear that the person is not making an effort. It is a hard concept to grasp that a person of any intelligence may have sudden sharp dips in areas of thinking. This is apparent in people with dyslexia. The person may fall into any ability range, may be well educated and successful, and yet be unable to read and write at the level of an average child. This sharp dip in ability to understand and learn happens for those with ASD on social and behavioural issues, so that their ability in this area may be on a par with or below a child's.

As a teacher I find that once this disability is acknowledged. it makes sense of some of the enigmas surrounding ASD behaviour as they struggle to learn social mores.

To illustrate this, look at the following and try to memorize it:

812241815 8161815158 2312 13127 2322522151311
13267692615152 261323 152226913181320 242613 2522
23212118246157

Being able to learn depends on many factors. The amount of information affects whether we can recall it, as does the logicality of the sequence. I could recall this if there were fewer digits and could recall a longer sequence if I saw a pattern, for example if it went up in fives – 510152025.

Look at this sentence and try to memorize it.

Social skills do not develop naturally and learning can be difficult.

Most will find that this can be memorized more easily than the number sequence. Each number in the first sequence corresponds to a letter in the second. The information is basically the same and in each case logical, but the second we learn far more easily because it fits out natural way of thinking.

You may have cracked the code yourself. If I now tell you that each number represents a letter of the alphabet in backwards sequence, so that

A=26 and so on until 1=Z. You could now probably reproduce the number sequence; but how long would it take you to painstakingly work through the information to do so? The difference between the time and effort needed to learn and reproduce the first sequence and those needed for the second gives an idea of the extra time and effort needed by a person with ASD to process and respond to a social event or to assimilate social mores.

Now consider this.

152226913181320 812241815 8161815158 188
231821218246157 268 719222 2312 13127 23225221513II
266712142671824261515 2

What is your reaction? For some it will be panic – 'No not numbers again!' For some it will be despair or annoyance – 'Do I have to work through another problem?' Some enjoy the challenge of puzzles, but even if you are one of those I doubt you would be happy tackling this if everyone around you was able decode this instantaneously. Imagine facing situations like this over and over again: frightening, upsetting and causing you far more effort than everyone else. What would you self-esteem be like? How would you cope with the stress?

Did you realize that the second number sequence is basically the same as the first? Each uses the same code pattern and the second reads, 'Learning social skills is difficult as they do not develop automatically'. Obviously the two sequences are very similar – or was it obvious to you? It is often puzzling to those working with people with ASD, as to why they repeat the same inappropriate behaviours. Donna Williams (1992) in her autobiography tells how she was reprimanded for writing on a wall. How was she to know that writing in a different medium in a totally different place constituted the same offence as making graffiti? Those offering support need the knowledge that what may appear a similar situation to most of the population can look like a completely dissimilar one to a person with ASD. An understanding of this will explain why a person repeats an inappropriate behaviour, having been remorseful and promising not to.

Anyone could learn this code. Depending on a person's ability level and the amount they practise, any person could become fairly efficient. Very, very few people could reach the stage where they could recognize the meaning as quickly as they could if it were written in normal script. It would take time and practice. It is equally difficult for a person with ASD to crack the social code despite any level of ability in other areas.

The message for the person offering support is *be patient*. He needs to be prepared to repeatedly discuss what may seem the same situation. The person with ASD is not being deliberately awkward if he appears to repeat the same inappropriate behaviour. This model explains why an individual can 'know' the correct behaviour, but act inappropriately. He has been taught the principles and can discuss what the correct response should have been. However, just as we could not look at the sequence of numbers shown above and in that moment recognize their meaning, neither could he in the heat of a real-life situation know the correct behaviour.

To establish the link discussion is needed of similar situations (repeatedly), with praise when they are correctly dealt with and a clear explanation of where mistakes happen. In some circumstances, an agreed consequence may be of value. For example, if the individual has kept his neighbour (and himself) awake by playing loud music, perhaps the system should be disabled so that no music can be played for an agreed number of nights. It is vital to use the strategy discussed earlier of making explicit why the behaviour is important. An acceptance and understanding that what is obvious to 99 per cent of the population may not be to this individual (even if he understands genetic engineering and/or can compose a symphony in his head) enables the person offering support to see why repeated explanation is necessary. We struggle to learn that for which we do not see the relevance. Most of us would put little effort into becoming proficient at using the number code, because it has no practical application for us. If we were given a reason, such as this has to be used to ensure privacy for some information or all employees who do not know it will be dismissed, we would be more likely to learn. Repeated reinforcement of the practical reasons for behaving in a particular way is essential.

People with ASD can, and do, learn social skills, but this does not happen naturally as it does for most. Anyone offering support should be aware of the problems and the need for specific strategies. As with anyone learning a difficult skill, the learner will make mistakes. Whilst not ignoring or condoning the behaviour, those giving support will be prepared to make allowances for this and not react as they would to an NT. More problematically, as will be discussed, there is a need for others who the person comes into contact with to do so.

In short:

- Problems in social skills are inherent in the condition of ASD.

- Areas where these are likely to put people at risk must be identified.

- If the risk cannot be avoided, strategies must be put in place.

- A person with ASD will need to painstakingly work out an appropriate social response.

- He will not spontaneously recognize similar situations and so will not transfer behaviour.

- He will not necessarily be able to apply in practice what is known in theory.

- Clear explanations and reasons are needed.

- Patience is necessary and the acceptance that, although the person with ASD can learn, social behaviour will never be automatic.

CHAPTER 8

Health Matters

Physical

Difficulties with daily living skills already described mean that individuals may need support to maintain a healthy lifestyle. They may wish to eat healthily, exercise regularly and so on, but be unable to regulate this and support can promote the necessary management. Although autism spectrum disorder (ASD) does not cause obvious physical difficulties, there are some problems and oddities that are prevalent amongst many people affected by this which affect support requirements. They may be poorly coordinated and clumsy.

Often, people with ASD do not appear to have the same awareness of physical sensation as most. John frequently does not register pain. My first consciousness of this was when as a child he was playing and I noticed blood running down his leg from a graze on his knee. He was oblivious, but when I asked him what he had done he looked in amazement at his leg and began to scream and cry loudly. Cuts, splinters, injections, even driving a garden fork through his own foot, have brought no reaction. I had thought this simply a peculiarity of his before learning that it is common to people with ASD.

There are similar problems with other sensations, such as heat and cold. Just as people with ASD may be hyper- or hypo-sensitive to information received through the senses, this seems to apply to these bodily sensations. With John, it sometimes simply appears that the processing is very slow. He would be impervious to cold, but then suddenly go from feeling nothing to crying because his frozen fingers hurt. If he dresses for a chilly morning, he will not remove layers when the sun comes out; if dressing in a centrally heated house, he will not add clothes to go out. The person offering support should be aware of the need to warn of temperature changes and alert the person to a possible need to react. A warning may provoke an overreaction in the person who is hypersensitive, but it is important not to be alarmed by this and have practical solutions at the ready.

The person may need support to monitor food and drink intake. Poor organizational skills cause difficulties in this area, but it also appears that many people with ASD do not recognize the sensation of 'being full'. Given a source of food and drink, such as a buffet, they will return again and again. At the social club John attends, some people will simply never refuse the offer of a drink, downing one after the other (fortunately all the drinks are non-alcoholic). Others will be over-fastidious, insisting on a restricted diet.

Temperature, food and drink are monitorable and it is the inability to recognize pain that is more difficult to develop strategies for. The combination of ASD tendencies makes describing symptoms almost impossible. The pain has to be recognized, located, the severity assessed, described in words and time parameters given. As with anyone, physical and emotional pain overlap and affect each other, but for a person with ASD the boundaries are even more blurred. They may be unable to differentiate between sadness and illness. All the person offering support can do is listen carefully, rely on medical checks and be aware that the problem may be emotional.

Once an illness is diagnosed, it is a fact which it is hard for rigid thinkers to let go of. John will continue to experience the pain when the indications are that he has recovered. Sometimes the only thing to do has been, once the visible symptoms have gone and test results are clear, to tell him that he is now better and expect him to return to normal daily routines. This can seem unkind when he continues to complain of being unwell, but it will usually bring a quick 'recovery', whereas he otherwise continues to believe he is, and to feel, ill. It is a strategy to be used with caution, and careful checks must be made so that actual illness is not overlooked. However, properly used it can relieve unnecessary suffering.

There is some evidence that people with ASD suffer gastric disorders. Several display symptoms of irritable bowel syndrome, which is influenced by stress.

The confusion over pain and symptoms is highly problematic. Those offering support need to make medical staff aware of the person's ASD, if they do not know, and to keep in mind the effects.

In short:

- ASD impairs the recognition of physical sensation, such as temperature and pain.

- The person may be hyper- or hypo-sensitive.

- The person offering support can monitor temperature and dietary intake.

- It is extremely difficult for a person with ASD to recognize and describe physical symptoms.

- He may not recognize the disappearance of symptoms.

Case study 8.1: Mark

Mark's story, told by his mother, demonstrates the emotional strain of having ASD. Each day is a struggle to attempt to understand and conform to social expectations. Changes such as the new store layout at work add to Mark's stress levels. Acute sensory perception causes difficulty with loud noises. His tenacity and courage enable him to work full time. However, his mother says that the level of emotional support needed takes its toll on the family. Mark's support profile can be found in Appendix 1.

Mark   *Mark is in full-time employment, and lives with his parents. This account is written by his mother, Lyndsey.*

My son Mark is 29 years old, and due to his cycling, hill walking and physical job is very fit. At just under six feet tall, he is a good-looking young man. For the past ten years, he has a full-time job as a customer assistant at a local supermarket. He drives his own car to work, having passed both the theory and practical driving test at the first attempt. He is a member of a young people's rambling club, cycles locally by himself and loves eighties and nineties music best, but also some current stuff – especially girl bands!

Watching him drive off in the morning he looks like any other young chap, which in many ways he is. However, we know the guts it may have taken, depending on the day, for him to go out and cope with work.

After we had consulted an educational psychologist, Mark attended mainstream primary school with a statement providing ten hours of support a week. This was invaluable, but, knowing what I know now, I would have done better to be pressing for a trained person in class and more input from the psychologist to help the school design support for Mark in dealing with specific problems.

Always a shy, solitary child, he had many phobias and fears, which at that time were not understood to be connected to his disability. He was extremely fearful of any loud noise particularly sudden ones, and was traumatized every time the school had a fire alarm check or there was a thunderstorm. This resulted in him then being worried just in case the alarm might go off or that it might thunder, and this fear remains to this day. Mark has taught himself coping strategies to help hide it at work, but specialist input from an early age would have been useful.

After much research into what was on offer for Mark at secondary school level and visits with him to the mainstream schools, we decided that the support available was not sufficient and he would be at risk of bullying. We felt that a local special school would best meet his needs The school provided for children from pre-school to 16, some of whom had behavioural difficulties. Staff were trained to work with pupils, who had general moderate learning difficulties and the staff to pupil ratio was much higher than in mainstream schools. The school was the 'best worst' option, and not ideally suited to his needs. However, his psychologist said at the time, 'short of opening my own school for youngsters like Mark there is no alternative'.

Outside the safe school environment, it was a different matter. Mark was fair game for some local boys who homed in on his 'different-ness': his extreme shyness, inability at ball games, immaturity and difficulty with social interaction. He just wanted to join in, but they would abuse him verbally and laugh at him. As he grew into a teenager, he became more isolated and so spent a lot of his time riding his bike locally. Even this was seen as a threat by some, or an opportunity for some local youths who would taunt him, chase him and even physically attack him.

On one occasion we reported an incident to the police, but they did little to help the situation. There was no appreciation from them that someone like Mark is open to be being abused physically, verbally and mentally. Instead of a 'shrug of the shoulders', the bullying of vulnerable people should be treated the same as racism and should be included in police 'diversity' training.

As part of a course at the local college, Mark went on work experience placements, one of which led to his current job. The manager of the store offered Mark full-time employment knowing about his learning disability and with the awareness that he would never be able to do certain jobs because, he said, 'He's a good hard-working lad'. Mark struggled to deal with the demands of the job, which initially was shelf stacking. He takes a while to get the hang of a task, and is meticulous about doing it right. This is not always what is needed, and speed is often more important. Recently the store was increased in size massively and had a second floor added so that stock locations were constantly changing. For someone with ASD who finds change difficult to deal with this was hugely stressful.

Mark needs instructions to be given clearly and only a few at a time. He is very conscientious and, once he has learned a task, will do it very well. However, he needs his superiors to be aware of his needs, and, with high staff turnover, information may not be passed on so this does not always happen.

Bullying takes many forms and Mark is vulnerable to being 'set up'; he is not streetwise at all. He has been called names, had jokes played on him and had foul things written on his car, usually by his peers. Again it's his 'different-ness'; he wants to be one of the lads, but finds small talk virtually impossible and does not pick up on non-verbal clues. He does not realize when he is boring on the subject of say, trains or eighties music.

These issues affect Mark deeply and he gets very down. He so wants to be like other lads, to go out with girls and just enjoy life. It is as if he knows where he wants to go, but has no compass or map to get there. As his parents we try to help him deal with situations that arise at work and with his feelings. Mark is gentle and his only recourse is to ignore bullying, rise above it and carry on. That takes very real courage and Mark has done it many times.

Mark blossoms if he gets a word of praise for a job well done, but in a busy store with not enough staff this is not going to happen very often. Inevitably, sometimes he gets things wrong and he has to be told. He is always mortified and remembers every negative word said to him, probably forever. His employers are good, but cannot be expected to have specialist knowledge of ASD. It is left to us to help him stick himself back together again, to face work the next day. Since his employers have been made aware of his ASD and were provided with specific information about his needs, improvement has been in evidence.

Mark copes very well with all that life throws at him, but it has taken a toll and he has been on anti-depressants for a few years now. His lack of self-esteem and difficulty in social groups are continuing issues; he still finds it difficult to talk to his peers. He is much better than he used to be with family and older people, and will engage in conversation. This still tends be only on topics that interest him and can develop into a monologue. His sense of humour has developed, so that he will laugh when we pull his leg about people's eyes glazing over – but he still keeps talking!

It takes its toll on us as Mark needs a lot of emotional support to help him deal with things. We spend much time supporting him to talk through his feelings, as well as helping with the practical issues.

Mark was finally diagnosed with ASD when he was about 23, although we had been aware that he had many of the classic traits. Mark found the diagnosis difficult to cope with and hated being given a 'label'. A big plus has been that he has met other young men and women like himself. His psychologist, who first diagnosed ASD, has been a great source of help and support for both Mark and us. Support from the NHS psychology service ended when she left. She, however, still supports us on a voluntary basis and has helped us, with a group of other parents, to set up our own social group for adults with ASD. This is a safe social setting, whereas as there was nothing in our area before. Mark enjoys attending regularly, although he still finds it hard to talk to his peers even there.

The support that Mark needs emotionally means that we only have one week a year away on our own, which is made possible by the support of his sister, her husband and good neighbours. Mark worries a lot about his health, and can fly into a panic if he feels sick or finds a spot in a place that he's not had one before. He needs to be talked through his panic and calmed down. If we are not here his sister takes over. This reassurance and talking over issues (the same ones time and time again), like work worries, lack of friends and trying to explain other people's actions, is constant.

An aspect often overlooked is the impact one sibling's disability has on another. Mark's only sister has willingly done her best to help, but we do not want that to be a burden; she has her own life to lead. We take other holidays with Mark, but he is becoming increasingly aware that it is unusual for someone of his age to be on holiday with the 'olds'; he should be with younger people not us. If we were not here, Mark would not have a holiday as he does not have any social groups to go away with who would understand his needs. He went for a weekend with his walking group a couple of years ago, but it was not a success for him. He looks like anyone else and is a pretty fit, capable walker, *but* he finds the social chitchat and the unspoken rules that we all know by a sort of osmosis to be like a foreign language. To be comfortable he needs to be with people who understand him, but don't patronize him – and that's a hard one.

He is a good very safe driver, but is only comfortable driving familiar short routes. He would not be able to drive off somewhere with a map and read road signs, but has to know the route intimately. He does not understand money very well; he copes with familiar things, like how much he needs for work, but has a tendency to take the exact amount he thinks he needs, forgetting that emergencies may arise.

This brings me to the future and what it will hold for Mark. We have always hoped that we will see him settled in his own home, whilst we are still fit and able to support him. Looking at the options available, this looks unlikely at the moment. Mark himself varies, from wanting to be like other lads of his age and not living at home with Mum and Dad, to saying that he's not sure he would like it. I think he would be very lonely in a flat of his own, especially if it was not very near to people that he knows well.

There would be emotional and practical issues: on the practical level Mark is very orderly and organized, but he would not be able to manage his finances without a lot of support. His cooking skills are limited, but could be improved with practice. The main problem for him would be worry about if something is cooked properly. He once had a tummy upset after eating a burger and knows about chicken and salmonella, so can get very panicky about that. Mark needs a high level of reassurance in many areas of his life in order to go out there and be the lovely helpful young man who assists with your shopping.

In an ASD friendly world what would I want for Mark and the other young people at our Tuesday Evening Social Club (TESC)? Sheltered/supported flats, where each person had their own front door but some communal areas where they could socialize if they wished. Shared laundry facilities and someone on call 24/7 whom they could contact if they had a problem. Each person would have their own supporter at whatever level they needed them, to help them with finances, personal issues and offer any necessary support. Not such a pipe dream really, as this sort of accommodation exists in many areas for people over 55.

Psychological stress

When we consider what the person with ASD has to deal with it is not surprising that they are prone to suffering stress, which can lead to bouts of depression. I feel that the world must often be a frightening place for them. We can usually predict with some degree of certainty what will happen in a given situation. But what does a person with ASD see? How frightening must it be to not be able to interpret what is around you? Most of us imagine it would be terrible to be deprived of a sense, to be blind or deaf; but how dreadful also to have these senses and to receive everything as a jumbled mass of data.

How wearing to be constantly struggling to make sense of the confusion. How disappointing to do your best at work only to be shouted at. How terrible to think you are having a pleasant chat and joke with friends to suddenly realize these people are in fact laughing at you. It is for me the stuff of nightmares where anything is possible. Friends can become monsters; nothing is stable or to be relied on.

All the support measures discussed aim to make life more comprehensible and manageable by introducing stability, interpreting events and offering reassurance. Relevant support is the mainstay in reducing stress, but it remains impossible to imagine how hard life with this disorder is. Neurotypical people (NTs) are as lacking in empathy towards people with ASD as vice versa. The first step in offering support is to attempt to appreciate the strain of living with ASD. Ideally the person offering support will be willing to put aside all prejudgement, and attempt to see the situation from the perspective of the person he supports, but this is a monumental undertaking. It is likely to take a person who has lived with an individual with ASD for many years, or an experienced psychologist or counsellor with much practical experience of the condition to begin to do this.

A basic requirement of offering support at times of stress is to stay calm. At times of crisis or difficulty, professionals have the advantage over family or informal carers, who may be caught up in whatever is causing the anguish. It is, however, not easy to remain uninvolved and unaffected by a tense situation. Professional support workers have the advantage in ensuring that they retain balance and distance.

In other instances concerns may appear trivial or illogical to an NT perspective. It is important not to dismiss concerns, because if not dealt with they will grow. Any issues raised have to be considered. We are locked into our own perspective, so that the university tutor will listen carefully and offer advice on academic matters, but is unlikely to take on board a student's concern about background noise that is unnoticed by others or his difficulty finding the lecture theatre. It is vital to be open to hearing and reacting to the unexpected. When we enquire how a person managed in a certain situation to ascertain his needs, we have preconceptions about how he may answer and what the needs may be. I asked someone how his new job was going and was told repeatedly about a broken shoe lace. His need at that point was for support in how to cope with what he saw as a crisis. It is easy to dismiss this, and say he is getting on fine if all he is worried about is his lace, but the fact is that this is what matters to him. Ideally the role of the person giving support is not merely to ensure task completion, but to be aware of the person's needs. These are easily overlooked when others see larger issues, but it is identifying the matters important to the person with ASD that is key to successful support. Dealing promptly with the problem of the shoe lace is likely to be a major factor in the success of the work placement. In the ethos of positivism, meetings to discuss progress are liable to focus on achievement, and give little attention to a problem that is generally seen as minor. If, however, it is major to the individual his worry will only increase as he is told it is of no concern, and it is not discussed and dealt with. The level of importance given must be in relation to the anxiety it raises, and not the perceived importance of the trigger. So in this instance serious discussion is needed between the person offering support and him about footwear – should he have spare laces, switch to Velcro® fasteners and so on – so that he can concentrate on elements that his employer and others view as more important in his dealings with them.

Differences in perspective bring about misunderstanding when the person offering support believes he has solved the problem. People with ASD are frequently labelled as awkward and unappreciative. Communication difficulties may result in the well-meaning supporter implementing something that he believes meets the person's needs, whilst the person with ASD actually feels his views have been entirely disregarded. A friend approached her support worker in college to request extra help on work placement. The tutor interpreted it as her being stressed by the work situation and offered a lower-level course without a placement requirement. The student had had trouble processing the information presented to her, and was distressed to realize that she was moved from the course she wanted on to one well below her capabilities. She was keen to master the work element and wanted only support. The tutor put much effort into arranging the change of course and felt unappreciated when the student did not return. Hard as it is the person offering support needs to consider that, if the recipient is not happy with what is offered, it is possible he did not really understand what the original problem was.

The solution may in fact be fine, but it has not been assimilated by the person. Decisions, especially by large organizations such as Social Services, are not usually implemented quickly. Discrepancies are inexplicable to ASD's rigid thinking. My son's social worker listened to his views about staying in his own house rather than moving to a flat and this was approved. However, some carers did not receive the information that he was not moving or were uncertain of the situation, and some were convinced he should move. Consequently they continued to talk to him about the flat and did not give the support he wanted to make the house his own. Although the reality of the situation was that he was to stay, John's perception was that he was liable to be forced from his home. Not surprisingly this made him extremely anxious. The person needs reassurance and for those offering support to be clear about what has been agreed. If it is a future plan then the steps discussed in the chapter about planning should be used, to reassure the person that it will actually happen.

The rigidity of AS thinking and the tendency to obsess means that a worry can escalate and dominate a person's life. Some fears may be related to hypersensitivity to sensory stimulation, such as Mark's (see Case study 8.1) fears related to loud noises. What Matt (see Case study 2.1) describes as irrational fears, such as putting his head under the shower or lighting matches, may also be a product of heightened sensory perception. A person may become phobic, with an extreme reaction which can be triggered by even the remotest possibility of contact with the subject. It is vital that there is an awareness of rising stress levels and prompt action. It is much easier to calm low-level stress than to reverse the downward spiral, which results from it being left unchecked. There may be signs such as an increase in repetitive actions, repeatedly asking the same question or mood changes. John will also become more clumsy and his speech more stilted. Sensitivity is needed to indicators of stress and a prompt reaction is required.

The cause of stress is not always obvious. Most people have times when they are down, but are unable to identify why. When John is like this, I discuss explicitly and in concrete terms what is happening to him. How does he feel? One thing I do not do is suggest to him what the cause of his distress may be. If I did he might latch on to this, and it would stop the real cause of his anxiety coming to light. Care is needed to not to lead the person, but to listen attentively. Suggesting a reason could even awake a concern he had not thought of. Instead I focus on what can he do about it? I allow him plenty of time and space to answer. Together we look for solutions. I confirm that he wants to shake the computer. What will the result be? What would be a better option? I make suggestions from options I have seen work for him in the past. A walk? A bath? A cup of tea? Phoning his sister? Ideally the support plan will include strategies that work for the individual. As a basic rule of thumb, regular, familiar routines are better stress busters than a novel idea. A holiday, for example, is more likely to add to stress than relieve it.

Like other individuals, some people with ASD find their own ways of coping with stress. Some are universal, such as regular sleep, yoga or exercise. Others are more individualistic, such as the 'squeeze machine' used by Temple Grandin. She designed this based on the cattle press which she had knowledge of in her professional work with animals. The pressure which it applies physically reduces anxiety and relaxes her (Grandin 1995). An ASD trait is to use 'stimming', for example pacing, rocking, spinning. Some professionals stop any such activity if possible, but Donna Williams (1994) describes actually teaching a young girl to tap and hum as a calming technique. It is natural for all humans to use this strategy. Mothers rock babies, music soothes and people automatically tap, clap or dance to the rhythm. There is a tendency to stop 'stimming' as it can look odd, and is therefore rejected to 'normalize' behaviour. Some must be stopped because it is physically harmful, such as head banging. I used to stop John's hand flapping and twirling. I did this partly because it makes him appear strange and partly because it sends him into a remote state, where his behaviour can become erratic.

It can be a tough call to know how much to respect the individual's right to withdrawal to a private ASD universe, and how far he needs assistance to cope in the world he must live in. As John grew up, I discussed with him the effects of his spinning. This involves twirling round and round, shaking his head violently, whilst listening to music. He could agree that overall the effects are not good. He becomes disorientated; he says he feels dizzy, and others around find it is difficult to communicate with him. He rarely does it now, but when he does, I get his attention and he stops. It is a matter for individual consideration as to how effective 'stimming' is as stress relief. Against the benefits has to be weighed the effect on others, in that it can lead to ridicule and social isolation, and the effect on the person of making them remote. These are matters for discussion and working out with the individual.

Stress is very dangerous to people with ASD, because they are liable to panic and provoke a worse situation. It is a common reaction to stress that people become forgetful, distracted, clumsy and therefore likely to make mistakes or have accidents, which further increase stress. When stress is acute a person may lose control, become scared or angry and shout or lash out. All of these apply equally to the person with ASD, but the problems are exacerbated by their general confusion and lack of social awareness. An incident of loss of control in public can lead to police involvement and/or a misdiagnosis of mental illness.

Those offering support need to be aware of signs of stress generally and specifically for the individual they are with. There are unavoidable situations and events beyond control which are catastrophic. The solution at times of extreme or prolonged stress may be supervision until the person is able to self-regulate. Always a specialist should be involved at the earliest possible point.

In short:

- Attention is needed to the concerns of the person, no matter how trivial or irrelevant they appear.

- The problem should be identified as seen by the individual with ASD.

- Vigilance must be kept for indications that the person is becoming stressed.

- 'Stimming' may act as stress relief.

- Stress reactions will be more extreme for those with ASD than for the average person.

Psychological obsessions

Obsessive behaviour is a problem, because an obsession dominates some-one's life. People become a slave to it unable to enjoy other pastimes, and like addicts are anxious if unable to get the next fix. The behaviour may also have intrinsic problems, such as the autistic woman who felt compelled to spend vast amounts on shoes, driving her parents to bankruptcy and suicide attempts. My son enjoys music and his main obsession is buying CDs from a particular store. This became problematic when he moved into a shared house with care staff support. He became so fixated on having money for this purpose that he did not want to go out, to look after his appearance or in fact spend money on anything else. He became withdrawn, depressed and anxious.

The development of obsessions can be pre-empted by ensuring that the person with ASD maintains a regular lifestyle, with a balance of work and social activities. A watchful eye is needed for signs that an interest is turning into obsession. The earlier this is recognized, and a plan put in place to control it, the less likely it is to grow to the extent where it controls. Once an obsession is established, it is very difficult to break.

Considering John's problem with wanting to spend all his money and time on CDs, I realized it had never arisen when he was younger because naturally we bought his food and clothes, and paid for outings and any other expenses, whilst he simply had pocket money. This automatically limited the amount of CDs he could purchase, and other expenditure was taken care of. The essential ingredients were that there was order and restraints to keep the obsession within boundaries. To manage it we returned to this system. John and I worked out a budget. He understands the principle that bills must be paid and food bought as a priority. We then discussed other needs, and money was earmarked for travel expenses, clothes, outings and so on. As part of this process a set amount each week is allocated to spending on CDs. The programme of activity that he has during the week ensures that he does not have large amounts of unstructured time when he could shut himself away with the music.

Some obsessions are dangerous and could cause harm to the individual or others, so of course must be stopped. However, most are harmless (in moderation!), and the best support strategy is to plan how they can be accommodated into the person's life. Having a structured lifestyle means that limits are naturally set on the amount of time and money available for any interest.

Attention may then be given to the positive aspects. My son enjoys music and we have built on opportunities for him to expand this beyond listening alone in his room. He has acted as DJ at a few events, even played one gig on local community radio, and is a star when it comes to the music section of the pub quiz. It is an interest he shares with many people (especially in his age group) and so gives a topic of conversation. If he wants to buy another CD, the answer is not, 'No you can't,' but, 'You will have enough money for this on Friday.'

He still buys at the same store despite people telling him he can buy cheaper elsewhere, or could download it from the Internet, and he duplicates singles and compilations with the same music. People are trying to help by telling us how could save money by changing his buying habits, but as I see it visiting this shop and selecting his CD gives him great pleasure. It may be slightly more expensive, and he may duplicate music, but this is within his budget and does no harm, so there are no benefits to John in changing. Again his perspective is different from most people's, but there are enough instances where the person with ASD has to modify behaviour to fit society, and there is no point changing something if there are no adverse effects for anyone.

In short:

- Obsession can lead to many problems for the individual and family.

- A structured lifestyle pre-empts the development of obsession.

- If not harmful, an interest can be built into normal lifestyles and routines.

- Positive aspects can be built on.

- There is no point trying to change behaviour that does no harm to the individual or others, simply because this is the way others think is best.

PART THREE

IMPLEMENTATION AND MANAGEMENT OF SUPPORT

CHAPTER 9

Managing Support

Planning

Parents have differing priorities and styles of parenting. They have priorities about knowledge and experiences they want for their children, and ideas about standards of behaviour. This is rarely formalized, but when such matters are discussed it is generally found that aims exist and parents have methods they hope work towards achieving these. As children become adults, this becomes more a matter for negotiation with the child gradually assuming responsibility for himself. When I am with other parents whose adult children have autism spectrum disorder (ASD), I find that like myself they have together developed specific strategies for dealing with particular situations. When professional support is involved, the planning becomes formalized to ensure it has aims and is constructive and that efforts are coordinated.

The mix of informal and professional support we draw on on a daily basis depends on a number of factors, such as the ability, age, health of the individual and varying circumstances. Few people receive support solely from either informal sources or solely from professionals. Most access professional services, even if only occasionally, and those receiving full-time professional care often also receive support from family and friends. Where there is a mix of support there will be formal planning by the professional service which may involve those offering support informally. Support for those with ASD will be most effective when it is planned cooperatively between the individual and all giving support. Planning is a requirement of professional support, but it has benefits for informal support. When my son was young I had targets for his behaviour. These were not written down or formally measured, but there were priorities. This not only helped him, but also helped me to notice, and be encouraged by, improvements. As described in previous chapters a more formal structure to organizing daily living is useful for people with ASD.

Planning clarifies the broad aims, from which goals can be set and monitored. Support empowers the person receiving it, when it is tailor-made to fit that individual's needs and he can see results. From the outset he needs space to explore personal requirements. In cases where support has a specific focus, for example finding employment, certain aims and methods may be indicated, but this does not mean that these will be the same as for another person in the same situation. There needs to be negotiation between the individual, those offering support, informally or professionally, and others involved, such as family members, employers, tutors and other agencies. Empowerment for the person with ASD comes from being actively involved, from initial planning through all stages of the support process.

ASD affects every aspect of a person's life, and, where support is general rather than to meet a particular goal, priorities will have to be set to decide which areas are to be tackled. There may be clear concerns that have to be addressed urgently, because the person is at risk. It may be that lack of concentration creates practical hazards, and often lack of social understanding makes the person with ASD particularly vulnerable in certain situations. Other goals will then be clarified by considering why the support has been requested, through discussion with the person and possibly family, friends and/or professionals, such as teachers or employers. Only a certain number of goals can be worked on. This holds true for anyone, but, for a person with ASD, the amount it is possible to work on effectively at any one time is likely to be small. As with any support programme, it is better to begin with few goals and succeed, than attempt many and achieve nothing.

When professional support is involved a plan is a vital working tool. From it routines are developed for daily practice. It is essential that this is then monitored. Paperwork should be related to the aims and kept as clear and immediately accessible as possible. For straightforward practical tasks this may be a simple tick chart. Besides keeping writing to a minimum, it focuses attention and ensures different carers follow the same pattern. From the perspective of the person being supported a completed chart may promote their sense of achievement.

The information collected should be summarized in a standard format that gives clarity about progress made towards specific goals, and which also highlights and quantifies any emerging concerns. The frequency of reviews will vary according to circumstances, but for anyone needing a high level of support a full review by management is essential at least once a month.

In short:

- Constructive support empowers the person with ASD.

- Support needs clear aims that are communicated to all involved.

- Workable goals need to be set and monitored.

- Management has responsibility for ensuring the plan is carried out and continually reviewed.

- Management ensure that the plan remains relevant and meets the person's current needs and wishes.

The specialist

The specialist is key to support. It cannot be reiterated too many times – ASD is a complex condition. An individual who seeks support, for example at work or college, may find this only increases stress if the person is unable to appreciate the problem from an ASD perspective. The person offering support needs be able to recognize the importance that a seemingly trivial matter may have, the difficulties experienced and the potential for misunderstandings. Effectiveness of support is maximized by direction from a specialist in this field.

The specialist is a person who has both theoretical and practical expertise. Theoretical knowledge is essential for having not only an awareness of how to deal with what arises on the day, but also a knowledge of how this fits into the overall programme of support. A person offering support may appear skilful in keeping the individual happy and meeting his needs whilst he is with him. However, if this does not fit with the overall pattern of support, it can be building up problems in the longer term. For example, a person with obsessions may be persuaded to do what all believe is the appropriate action in return for a reward related to the obsession. This may be seen by daily supporters as good practice, but the specialist will know that this feeds the obsession and is therefore not supportive in the longer term. The obsession may be harmless in itself. For example it may be buying a particular item or playing a computer game, but as discussed in Chapter 8, obsession is dangerous to mental health. Using it as part of the support offered is the equivalent to giving an alcoholic a drink as part of his programme. In the early stages he will meet other targets for the reward, but ultimately the outcome is likely to be disastrous. The analogy is not so clear to the person offering support, who offers something as intrinsically harmless such as an extra trip to the store. The specialist is needed to remind him that the supporter's role is to work towards longer-term objectives and this may mean disagreeing with the immediate wants of the individual with ASD.

Practical experience is essential. This has to be hands-on, practical experience of day-to-day support. It is impossible to have an understanding of ASD from theoretical study alone. In order to be able to design and implement effective support, the person must develop the skill of listening to and working with people with ASD. This means spending time with people in a range of daily situations. Professionals may have a skewed experience if they meet people only in an artificial, for example clinical, setting, and if the only interaction centres around a specific aspect or problem. They need to be fully aware of the person as an individual, with his own talents, aspirations and desires. This calls for practical knowledge of the situations the person faces regularly and of their effect on him. Day-to-day experience over an extended period is essential too, in order to recognize the unrelenting nature of the disorder. Reports of major events do not chronicle the multiplicity of minor details that create constant worry, or give insight into the sheer effort of living with ASD. To offer support, the specialist must recognize how mercilessly it batters away continually creating confusion and stress for the person. He needs to understand how this ripples out causing tension in those closest, and reaching to those who support regularly. This pressure frequently results in misunderstanding and dispute between the individual, families and professional supporters. All involved need the expertise of a specialist who can relate to the reality of the situation, whilst holding in mind the total picture.

In short:

- A specialist is key to giving effective support to people with ASD.

- The specialist must have both sound theoretical knowledge and intensive practical experience.

CHAPTER 10

Care Plan

Design

This is an example of a care plan that I drew up for my son. Although John is a tall, good-looking, generally physically fit young man, his autism spectrum disorder (ASD) causes him difficulty in all aspects of life. He is unable to organize and coordinate the completion of tasks unaided. His lack of social awareness leaves him vulnerable to others, and also means he may unwittingly offend or scare those who are unfamiliar with him. He requires support to be available at all times.

Not all people with ASD will need such high levels of support. Some may need professional support only at certain times, such as transitions or times of great stress. Some will need support in only one or two areas of daily living. In this chapter we will examine John's care plan. I hope that this will offer the reader ideas for aims and strategies that can be selected and customized for others with ASD to be used by those giving support informally or professionally.

Aims of the programme

To assist John to meet his aspiration to have as 'normal' a life as possible by:

- supporting and developing his social skills so that John is able to live safely in the community
- enabling him to have opportunities for employment and study, which give him a sense of achievement
- supporting him to develop leisure activities, which provide interest and enjoyment
- building independent living skills.

Rationale

With appropriate support, John can care for himself, live safely in the community and achieve satisfaction and pleasure from his accomplishments. He can relate positively to others, maintain his own home, carry out some part-time employment and enjoy leisure activities.

John does not have the organizational and social skills to live independently. Care must be maintained at an appropriate level or he will become increasingly disorientated, confused, depressed and a danger to himself and/or others.

The vital first step in any programme is establishing its purpose. It is easy to believe that everyone is working to the same end, whereas in reality those offering support are pulling in different directions. I had thought the aims I have set out above were universally accepted by the care team. I was shocked when a carer, coming to a section on a form about aims, made a comment to the effect that this was irrelevant and it was simply about making sure John was looked after. This first section of the plan sets the scene for all that underpins the support. It is not about ensuring John is minded, the house is cleaned, that he has some occupation and goes out; but about enabling him to cope more independently, to live safely, to achieve his aspirations and to enjoy himself.

Strategies

1. Identify areas of high risk and have risk assessments in place.
2. Provide a programme which keeps John physically and mentally active.
3. Ensure there is order and routine.
4. Give support to manage leisure time.
5. Set longer-term goals.
6. Monitor health.
7. Monitor for signs of stress.
8. Set goals for personal development.

Strategies can now be designed to meet the aims. The first strategy relates to the aim to live safely in the community, which is fundamental to the success of the plan. John's need for support is high at present. He is an active young man who would like to have a friends, and in particular a girlfriend. His lack of awareness of social boundaries means he may talk or act inappropriately.

Because of his size, this can be frightening for people who do not know him. He is then vulnerable to attack or arrest. Such behaviour is rare, but the consequences are so severe that 24-hour support is needed.

1. Identify areas of high risk and have risk assessments in place

The nature of John's disability means that the greatest area of risk is in social situations. John may make an inappropriate comment to a member of the public. His body language and eye contact may cause offence.

- Risk assessments should highlight particular risk areas, for example swimming pools, entertainment areas with large groups of people, work that involves contact with the public.

- John should have positive reinforcement of expected behaviour before going to such places.

- He should be closely supervised at all times in high-risk environments by staff who are both experienced and physically able to stay close to him. For example he should not be at a swimming pool with a non-swimmer or walking with someone who is unable to maintain a reasonable pace.

- Carers must be aware that certain stimulations, such as twirling on a dance floor, cause John to go into a state where he may be unable to control his actions. He should always be redirected to a more appropriate activity. When away from such situations, he does have an understanding of this himself and can recognize the need for this support.

- Carers must be aware of potential risks, for example people who have been drinking, young women, and either move John away or remind him of the appropriate social rules.

- Risk strategies should be regularly reviewed with professionals and family.

Risk assessment must be a high priority on any care programme. Those with ASD are vulnerable to bullying and abuse. Mark (whom we met in Case study 8.1) is a mild-mannered man, and yet bullies still persist in seeing him as a target. At times even he is provoked to retaliate, even if only verbally. If the person with ASD does fight back, they are likely to receive the blame as they will be less able to explain and justify themselves. Social naivety means they can be easily befriended by and used by the unscrupulous. Darren (see Case study 12.1), has many 'friends' when he has a car and money who will use him as a free taxi and supplier of drinks, but they disappear when he loses the car and needs favours returning. People with ASD find their own attempts at friendship can be misinterpreted, or their inappropriate approach may appear threatening. This is a particular concern for Harry (see Case study 6.1). Seeing a smart-looking middle-aged man, people have expectations which he may not fulfil. His childlike innocence and interest is incongruous with his appearance and so others may read motives into his words and actions which do not exist. Lack of social understanding, normal inhibitions or awareness may in a few instances lead to behaviour that involves police intervention. Unexpected change in surroundings or routine may cause the person with ASD to become distressed, and act in a way that appears strange or aggressive. Those offering support may become habituated to a person's behaviour, but the care plan must try to foresee the effect this could have in public places.

2. Provide a programme which keeps John physically and mentally active

This gives John a sense of well-being and achievement Without this he fixates on obsessions and becomes depressed.

- John will often need very explicit instructions for example rather than saying 'The kitchen needs cleaning', break it down into small tasks.

- It is not always clear to him how to do a simple task and detailed instructions relieve his stress. They also keep him focused on the task, which lessens the tendency to obsessive thoughts.

- Reminders as to why he is doing the job keep him motivated. John does not link cause and effect, and so may see no reason for doing a certain task. It is always good to automatically add a reason, for example 'The worktop must be wiped, so that it is clean to prepare food on. Otherwise we will have stomach ache and be sick.'

- Like anyone he has days when he does not want to work. Most of us see the bigger picture, and realize that we have to turn up for the day's work to earn a crust or must mow the lawn before it becomes a jungle. John often needs the reasons stating and regularly reiterating.

- He responds well to having someone alongside him. Using 'we' rather than 'you' can make a big difference. 'We need to get this room tidied' (rather than 'You need to tidy the room') – 'I am looking forward to our game of bowls' (rather than 'You are bowling this afternoon').

- It is important to stay positive. John tends to see things as good or bad. If he hears negative comments about any activity these will be amplified. We all know that we would rather be playing than working – but it is a mistake to say things to him such as, 'Let's hurry up and finish the housework and then we can go into town': such statements will make him increasingly negative about work. Instead a comment such as, 'We have two hours to do the housework, so we can make this place look really good, before we go into town', presents it in a far more positive light.

- John responds well to humour.
- Have a selection of activities that can be referred to on days when the normal routines cannot be followed, for example college holidays, papers not here for round, not well enough for set activity such as swimming.

The programme covers John's activities during the weekdays and so addresses the second aim. It is a mix of work for his therapeutic earnings, college, household routines and leisure activity. It is worked out jointly with him and support workers, and there is then agreement that it will run until the review date. This balances choice against the need for the stability of a fixed programme. It is vital that all concerned know how to motivate him, so that he maintains progress rather than suddenly realizing that he is failing to achieve his aspirations. Derek, an autistic adult, although in his fifties, is glad that his mother still holds this balance for him. He lives with her and works part time on a supported programme. He acknowledges the benefits of this placement, and the need to complete household chores, but knows he has neither the organizational skills or concentration to complete these without her support.

3. Ensure there is order and routine
This gives John a sense of purpose and provides security.

- Follow the programme.
- Differentiate between programme time – daytime Monday to Friday – and free time.
- Follow personal hygiene routines. John needs reminders about cutting toenails as well as daily routines.
- Check regularly that he has toiletries and help him to replace these as necessary.
- Ensure John puts things away, clears kitchen after meals, cleans spillages and so on. Use the methods described above to motivate

him. He may not volunteer to do these things, but becomes unhappy if the house is out of order.

- Tidy cupboards regularly. John bungs things away and then is distressed he cannot find things. Also he mixes dirty cleaning materials with food in kitchen.

- Ensure meal times are regular.

- Ensure that John maintains a regular sleep pattern.

Order and routine is useful to many people; vital for those with ASD. These elements run through all aspects of the programme. This is the basis to providing a sense of security and pre-empting problems. Sarah lives alone and supporting routines for running the household is a necessity. Setting a menu for the week with shopping times and lists built in overcomes the problems she had of rotting food in the fridge.

4. Give support to manage leisure time

John does not find free time easy. He finds it hard to maintain friendships, and to decide on a leisure activity. He enjoys a range of activities, such as cooking, drawing and board games, and likes outings and social gatherings, but left to his own devices will listen to music for hours. Whilst music is good as a hobby, it is not good for his mental health when it becomes obsessional.

- Encourage John to engage in a range of interests at home.

- Support John to organize meetings with friends.

- Ensure that his computer and other electrical leisure equipment functions. This means supporting him to maintain equipment, for example replace ink cartridges in printer, clean video heads, and to replace as necessary.

- Support him to organize outings.

Leisure time is often not easy for those with ASD and this relates to the third aim. An individual may cope well during structured work time, but identify using free time as the aspect of their life where support is needed. Adults such as Harry and Mark, who are successfully working full time, have their days occupied but can find themselves at a loss to know how to occupy leisure time. Many enjoy organized activities, but do not appear to have the imaginative skills to initiate these independently.

5. Set longer-term goals

This ensures John has interests, something to work towards and look forward to. This can be any sort of project from shopping for clothes, decorating a room, arranging a day out or cooking a meal for someone, to planning a college course.

- Support is needed to ensure the project progresses.
- Ensure there is continuity.

Many aspects of life require organization, which a fragmented ASD view of events renders impossible. Assistance with longer-term projects has to be integral to the scheme. People who mainly manage independently may require support with larger projects, such as decorating, planning a holiday or changing jobs. Emma (whom we will meet in Case study 16.1) works capably on a daily basis, but, when she became dissatisfied with the current job, needed much assistance to handle applying for and settling into a different one. Fortunately this was available and she is again happy in her work.

6. Monitor health

John is often unable to differentiate between physical pain and stress. His emotional state also affects his health and stress leads to bowel problems.

- Ensure John follows a healthy diet.
- Ensure meals are regular and eaten at the table.
- Encourage him to chew his food and not to rush.
- Encourage him to drink plenty of water – and limit tea or coffee.
- Check the toilet book daily.

As health is central to living a comfortable life for anyone, support with caring for it is basic to the programme. Confusion about the source of pain, and physical problems are common amongst those with ASD. John notes in the toilet book when he has been to the lavatory, as he would not otherwise be aware that he was becoming constipated. Like many with ASD, he can be confused about time. If an event causes anxiety he will imagine it has happened more frequently than it has in reality. Those offering support check the book and give medication as needed.

7. Monitor for signs of stress

John has difficulty identifying what is causing stress, even to the extent of being unaware if it is physical or emotional.

- Carers must be aware of any changes in behaviour. Changes may be, for example:
  - speech becomes more stilted and monosyllabic
  - increase in echolalia
  - speech returns more frequently to obsessive themes
  - overeating
  - throwing things away
  - breaking things
  - changes in sleep pattern
  - refusing to follow a routine
  - unwillingness to take part in social activity
  - hoarding.

- Any unusual and/or inappropriate behaviour should be picked up as soon as possible.

- The frequency of unusual and/or inappropriate behaviours must be monitored.

- A quick, immediate consequence should be given for any negative behaviour which will in itself increase stress, for example you have thrown this away, you must walk to the shop to replace it. A consequence must be unpleasant if it is to stop the behaviour – and unpleasant to John. He may, for example, have thrown something away so that he will get a car ride to Tesco to look at CDs! The consequence for this should then be a walk to a less appealing shop. John will be grumpy, but an appropriate consequence not only stops the problem escalating, but also alleviates his stress by demonstrating there are secure boundaries for him.

- Engaging in activity alleviates stress. This needs to be an activity that engages him mentally and possibly physically. He likes routine tasks that give a sense of accomplishment.

- Listen to John. It is best to do this in short bouts and in some instances at a pre-arranged time. It is hard for him to express his thoughts: he needs to have time to put his point together. Talking for a long time will in itself increase his stress.

Being stressed is not good for anyone, but as previously discussed is particularly dangerous for people with ASD. They can rapidly get into a downward cycle, which can even lead to self-harm. Stress can also lead to a breakdown in behaviour. One outbreak of uncontrolled behaviour can have extreme consequences, destroying years of achievement, and wiping out progress towards all set aims. The signs to watch out for need definition, careful monitoring and strategies in place, which can be implemented immediately there is any concern. The importance of this cannot be over-emphasized.

8. Set goals for personal development

John needs support for personal development, which will enable him to be more independent. Having more understanding and control of a situation also makes it less stressful for him.

- Select one or two goals from observation of, and in discussion with, John. The goal might for example be to be able to arrange a meeting with a friend, to meet a healthy eating target or to know how his budget works.
- The goal must be discussed and broken into easy, measurable steps.
- John must have opportunities to put learning into practice.
- Success, and the benefits of this, must be pointed out to him.

This final strategy looks to the longer term and to consolidating personal progress. Everyone develops and changes as they deal with new experiences. People with ASD do not learn spontaneously from events, but often need support to realize an effective way of tackling a situation. The value of lifelong learning is acknowledged in education, and it is increasingly recognized that in a changing world, people at every life stage need to acquire new skills. As for anyone lifestyle changes as the person with ASD ages, and they will face new challenges requiring them to adapt. Given discussion and systematic learning the person can build skills to work towards achieving current goals.

No matter what the quantity of support needed is, the quality of support will always need to be high. The programme will need specialist input at the planning stage so that it effectively meets recognized aims. The prime function of the support is to give psychological and emotional support, and thus to promote the ability to manage independently. Completion of physical tasks are only important in as far as they contribute to these wider goals.

It is important to remain focused on the aims of the programme and the rationale. It is this latter, which brings home the import of the scheme. For John as for many others, appropriate support is the difference between being unable to make sense of the world, living to the individual's true potential, rather than descending into chaos causing unhappiness and possibly harm to themselves and others. The difference is vast in terms of social and financial costs.

In short:

- Aims must be clearly stated.

- Any risks must be assessed and plan in place to implement as necessary.

- Strategies must relate to the programme's aims.

- Specialist support is needed to ensure strategies promote progress towards personal goals.

Implementation

Good strategies are the vital basis to support. However, the care plan does not end there. This section of it will set out measures to see that the ideas are tranlated into action. Implementation consists of four stages:

1. planning
2. communication and recording
3. monitoring
4. review.

Planning is essential, but only the first step in implementing the care plan. It is a living document which must be communicated to all concerned, so that they can carry it out. Managers take responsibility for checking that it is adhered to and regularly updated.

1. Planning
Planning has to be in place for each of the strategies listed above.

2. Communication and recording

Continuity and consistency are of great importance to John, as they are to anyone with ASD. Good communication and record-keeping are essential to achieving this. Some examples of possible records to keep are listed below. Recording systems should be clear and easy to complete (for example tick charts).

- *Checklist of daily routines.* For example, personal hygiene, meal times, routine for clearing up afterwards to be kept up to date and recorded.

- *Activity rota.* This should include timings, so that John knows, for example, that sweeping a mess under the carpet will not mean housework session is over in ten minutes – rather there will be other tasks until time is up. He will know too that he cannot manipulate to extend a more pleasurable activity, for example music mixing will not begin until the agreed time. This will relieve him of much anxiety.

- *Diet sheet.* A record of what John eats is necessary to ensure he has a healthy balanced diet. This should include some indication of amounts. To John, 'sandwiches' may mean a loaf of bread and pound of cheese.

- *Strategies and goals for personal development.* Record goals, motivators and success daily.

- *Signs of stress and action taken* (see strategy 7 on p.112).

- *Progress on long-term goals.* Staff must be aware of where he is up to with planning any project, so that even if they are not involved they can reassure him about where it is at.

- *Communications book.* The communications book is a 'catch all'. It is available to all involved to record any information that needs to be known, but it does not come up on the record sheets. It is generally for simple day-to-day messages and reminders.

Information must be clearly communicated so that staff are consistent in their expectations and approach. The reason behind the strategy needs also to be known. A person offering support may not understand the necessity for keeping to a routine; he may, for example think he is doing the person a favour by letting them miss a cleaning chore that they complain about, not realizing that the complaint was merely a learnt speech pattern and the result of not sticking to routine is a steady build-up of distress at the ensuing lack of order.

Anyone with ASD may inadvertently give a different story to different people, yet it is extremely important to the person that there is consistency from those giving support. This can only be achieved if the details are adequately communicated to all involved. This inevitably involves paperwork. This should obviously be kept to a minimum, because precious support time should not be swallowed up by it – and because if there is too much to plough through it will not be effective. Tick charts are a check that each step is carried out, but call for the minimum of writing. The information is quickly recorded and easily read. Measures of time and quantities are important, as different carers may put greatly different interpretation on what is appropriate. One may consider a quick wipe of the work tops constitutes cleaning the kitchen, whilst another interprets this as cleaning inside ovens and cupboards. Similarly with food, a bowl of cereal may be a basin-sized bowl full to the brim or a small bowl half full. Records must be kept daily to ensure that goals continue to be worked towards. Signs of stress must be recorded, as well as how this was dealt with. Any worrying signs or frequent occurrences of low-level indicators must trigger concern and bring in the specialist advisor. A communication book is for any information, which is important and not covered by record sheets.

3. Monitoring

- Management have a responsibility to ensure that all staff working with John are experienced and aware of the working procedures.
- If there is an emergency and staff who are less familiar with John must be used, management must ensure that they are briefed on the level of care (i.e. supervision at all times and John not to be left until there is another carer or family member to take over) and that adequate steps are taken to ensure his safety.
- Management should ensure there is adequate record-keeping and communication to ensure all strategies are fully implemented.
- Management should regularly check staff knowledge of routines.
- Management should spot check that routines are being carried out.
- Management should check the cleanliness of the home.
- Management should check John's appearance.
- All checks to be carried out at least once a month.

Managers assume the responsibility for seeing that the plan is fully and correctly implemented. Staff need to have appropriate training and be briefed about the individual needs. It may not be practical to pass on all details to a support worker called on to cover, but there is essential information that must be given to ensure there is no risk to the individual, the worker or others. The paperwork must be checked to see that all routines are followed and to discover any problems. Those offering supports may be isolated and become de-motivated or misunderstand the process. The management role includes spot checks that the routines are being followed correctly. A person with ASD may be unable to correlate the practicalities to the care plan to explain if there are discrepancies. He may recognize problems, but be unable to communicate these. Those with ASD, especially people who require high levels of support, are extremely vulnerable in a one-to-one care situation, because of the problems with formulating a complaint. Management, therefore, have a high level of responsibility to carry out regular, effective checks to ensure the programme is adhered to. Cleanliness of the home and a tidy personal appearance are not goals in themselves, but are indicative that the self-care and independent living goals are being met. Duty of care dictates that under no circumstances must there be a failure to carry out such checks, at a very minimum, each month.

4. Review

- John, family, carers and other professionals should take part in reviews.
- Aims and strategies to be reviewed six monthly or more frequently if necessary.
- Feedback from monitoring to be reviewed monthly or more frequently as necessary.
- All parties to be invited to contribute in writing and/or at meeting.

Regular reviewing is essential to ensure that the strategies are being effective in meeting the aims of the programme. A care plan can fail drastically if the broader aims are not kept to the forefront.

The agreed aims of the support programme for my son were around assisting him to have as 'normal' a life as possible, caring for himself and living safely in the community pursuing a mix of work, study and leisure activities. Two years on many of the staff supporting my son in his house still have no idea how his cooker works. Despite his desire to keep the house smart, there are grubby marks on walls and doors, several weeks' worth of dust on some surfaces and the grass has grown so that the lawn mower will not cope. His toenails are so long there are holes in his socks. The fridge that he asked for support to defrost is at the stage when it will soon run water, because the door no longer shuts. He would like to decorate, but the assistance needed to organize himself to do this is not forthcoming. Leisure activities are mainly with family, as support workers are unable to organize outings and meetings with friends, or to coordinate them with shifts which anyway finish at ten in the evening. Meanwhile John knows all about how things in the care agency office work. Not surprising, as he is taken there most days. He is an expert on staff rotas, even uses the office computer to type up lists of his own routines sometimes. He has his own pigeon hole and a whole new terminology of shifts, handovers and service users. The overall effect of support is that rather than workers coming into his world and supporting his life aims, John is sucked into theirs. This effect is not visible to individuals seeing only sections of support, and managers have the oversight to see that this misdirection does not happen to the programme.

Aims may need to be changed to fit changes in the individual's circumstances. Strategies will be modified as some cease to be relevant and emphasis needs to alter. The person, family and all professionals should be invited to contribute in the way that they find most comfortable. As previously mentioned, the person with ASD may be uneasy in a large meeting and must be offered alternate ways to put forward his requirements.

It is vital that the aims remain clear. The review must systematically appraise all elements of the plan in view of what it sets out to achieve and its effectiveness. It should not be sidetracked into looking at purely practical measures, which ought to be dealt with as a matter of course, or are not fundamental to promoting the aims. Its function is to ensure that all involved are carrying out their role, that strategies are followed and that they are effective in meeting the aims of the programme.

In short:

- An effective plan is communicated to all.

- Success depends upon strategies being monitored and recorded.

- Management have a duty of care to carry out checks to ensure the programme is followed.

- Regular reviews guarantee that strategies are followed, and that they continue to be relevant to the aims of the programme.

CHAPTER 11

Ethics

Ethical considerations are paramount when offering support, and must constantly be taken into account. I include ethics only at this late stage, because the practicalities of giving support must be studied in order to be aware of specific issues relating to the disorder. For the professional broad principles, such as the duty of care, respect for the individual and confidentiality, apply to working with people with autism spectrum disorder (ASD) as they do generally. Many people with ASD remain more susceptible to parental influence than the majority of their peers. Parents naturally feel more responsible for a child with ASD. My son needs support that my other adult children do not, but he must also be respected as an adult.

People with ASD can be very vulnerable, which creates many moral dilemmas in providing support. Parents, teachers and other adults make major decisions for children. It is a natural process that, as they grew older, they gradually take over responsibility for their own decisions. Aspects of ASD render it problematic for a person to comprehend various situations and make appropriate choices. Some people, like my son, would be totally overwhelmed by the complexity of managing everyday living. The support that he requires means taking over from him some responsibility for planning and budgeting, and consequently making some decisions that would normally be his.

An understanding of the communication and social problems intrinsic to ASD, indicates how difficult it is for the individual to communicate his needs and wants. It can be extremely difficult to ensure that support is in line with the person's wants and his best interests. All people with ASD, including the highly intelligent, are susceptible to being led by others and it is very easy for the person offering support, either knowingly or unwittingly, to lead the person down a route, which is not the course he wants to follow. There is an ethical responsibility on people managing support to ensure that the focus does not drift away from the needs of the user. Clearly targeted support must be regularly monitored and reviewed to ensure that it genuinely meets the needs of the person with ASD.

We have made much progress in care and rightly look to respect the right of all individuals to take control of their own life. A balance has to be struck between respecting a person's right to choose, and burdening him with options which cause confusion and distress, and may therefore ultimately be damaging to his mental health. Like several of his friends, my son does not have a strong grasp of numbers and cannot see how one decision impinges on another. This renders him incapable of managing his finances independently. John and I agree the theory that basic living costs such as food and bills must be met, but in practice I arrange this from his benefits. We then discuss other needs and wants to organize a budget for items such as clothes, activities and savings. The small amount of money that John controls completely independently causes him a disproportionate amount of worry. He wants to buy things and go places, but he also wants a large bank account. Don't we all? The difference is that most of us can weigh the options and will strike a compromise between spending and saving. John cannot and becomes very stressed. Ethically there must be supervision and controls to ensure the rights and well-being of the person are supported.

Inability to read social situations and a lack of ability to look beyond this moment in time puts people with ASD greatly at risk. Some people need support to regulate their behaviour. To ensure that my son's behaviour is stable, there are still boundaries in place and occasional sanctions. There are difficult ethical issues to face in managing the behaviour of an adult, and these must be considered at every stage. As I would with any pupil or student, I always discuss with John why it is necessary to follow a particular behavioural rule. He is a reasonable, kind and loving person, who would not deliberately hurt or offend. The problem is that teaching him about behaviour is like teaching a paraplegic person to drive a car. In the same way that they, after study, approached the theory but would be unable to drive a standard car, John can do the theory of behaviour, but in a practical situations simply cannot apply it. If he is taken step by step through a scenario, he will be able to work out what the consequences of particular behaviour would be and to decide how he should act. In a real-life situation with no guidance and surrounded by various sensory stimulations, he will be unable to analyse the problem. Even able-bodied learner drivers, despite knowing which pedal does what and having an understanding of traffic regulations, find that it is difficult to assimilate all the information and skills required to cause the car to drive smoothly in the required direction. Social situations are too diverse, complicated and move too fast for John to judge. Without some imposed controls, he would find himself (and possibly place others) in very distressing situations.

The alternative to behaviour management is to allow the behaviour and mental state of people like John to deteriorate until the only option is the one modern care practices set out to move away from and avoid: detention in an institution such as a mental hospital or prison. A lack of simple measures in the house John shared swiftly led to a breakdown. We then moved abruptly from a situation where it was unethical to take his radio from him to ensure a night's sleep, to one where he was locked up and terrified. Not to take steps to support behaviour must surely be immoral and a denigration of our social responsibility. It is the equivalent of strapping the person with physical disabilities into the car he cannot control. Society must apply reason in balancing the rights of the individual against a duty of care to those needing support.

My son is able to discuss difficulties that he has with behaviour. If the person is able to do so and can actively participate in planning interventions, this allows him control. If intervention is needed, it is planned with prior consent from the individual and can be discussed with him afterwards in relation to the plan. The situation then has parallels with a person planning to hand over control to a medical professional in the event of his being unconscious or otherwise incapacitated.

Ethical issues affect many aspects of care. The rights of an individual to make choices about his lifestyle must be balanced against his right to support which ensures that his disabilities do not adversely affect his welfare.

In short:

- The basis of ethical support is a duty of care, respect for the individual and confidentiality.

- There is an ethical responsibility on care managers to ensure that the aims for the person with ASD remain the focus of the support.

- Respect for the individual's right to autonomy must be balanced against the duty to care.

- Any behaviour management needs should be clearly discussed and planned with the person with ASD as far as is possible.

- Ethical considerations should be prioritized at every stage to ensure the rights of the individual are respected.

CHAPTER 12

Family Support

Caring for the family/carers

I watched with a heavy heart as, less than a year after he and I had put a great deal of effort into constructing it, John's computer desk was dismantled. The sturdy chipboard sides were smashed and the frame twisted, because of his frequent need to move it. He would have dropped something behind it or felt the urge to check the wiring. Eventually the support worker and I decided it wiser to take it down, rather than leave it to crash asunder smashing the computer with it. The washing machine was full, largely with clean washing, which had been thrown back into the basket and mixed into the dirty linen. Obviously all the reasoning as to why it was beneficial to iron and put clothes away properly had been forgotten that day, in favour of a quick, instant get-out.

Breakages and wastages are all hidden costs of the hidden disability. It added to my financial worries. John had only benefits; I had part-time work, which I made up to a living wage with supply teaching. I did not dare take on the commitment of regular full-time work on top of his care needs. Summer was coming, which meant this casual work would stop. My tiredness and stress levels spawned their own mini-crises. I needed to track down a supplier for a new salad box for the fridge. The previous evening I had absent-mindedly neglected to turn off the hob, and, running out of space on the work top, put the salad box on the smouldering gas ring. Fortunately John saw the flames and called me quickly.

As I contemplated our situation, I would have liked that great British solace, a cup of tea, but the large carton of milk I purchased the previous day was mysteriously empty in the bin.

This is a snapshot of a day in life with my son. It is difficult for a person who does not live with it to understand how wearing supporting a person with ASD can be. On the most basic practical level, it is the family who have no washing machine or TV when this has been fiddled with and broken. They have to organize and pay for the repair or replacement. It is the family who wake up to find all the milk intended for breakfast has been guzzled or perhaps poured away in order to recycle the bottle, who try to leave for work to find their keys have disappeared; it is their home and possessions that are damaged or lost. These are all trivial incidents in themselves, but not what an average person wishes to have to deal with regularly before or after a normal day's work.

My first experiences of being in a group of parents of children with disabilities left me feeling a complete fraud. Most children's difficulties were immediately obvious, whereas I floundered as parents asked me what disability did this little boy have, who looked so well, ran, played and chatted. We did not at that stage even have the label of ASD. There are many people with ASD, who have little outward sign of disability, but this does not mean it does not have a very real impact on their lives and therefore on their families.

At best life is ground hog day. One of the support workers suggested that this would be the ideal for a person with ASD – one single day that repeats itself over and over again. This for that individual is comforting, but for most of us repetition becomes tedium. Being asked to repeat yourself can be aggravating, but imagine what it feels like to be having the same conversation over and over again, day in day out, endless repetition. Then no matter how tired you feel or whatever the crisis, it is necessary to keep to a timetable. A friend describes how, in the midst of coping with a flooded house, a number one priority was setting up the ironing board so that her son's clothes were ready and his routine not disrupted.

There is the continual tension of coping with high stress levels. If my friend's son did not have ASD, I would say, 'Why the hell are you doing his ironing anyway?' Because he does I understand completely that doing this at a set time each week is a small price to pay for keeping down stress levels. John will be inordinately worried about what appears to everyone else as trivial, but our stress levels rise as we hear his anxiety and have to repeatedly answer the same questions. The problems are exacerbated at any time of crisis or excitement, that raises the already high stress levels. Just as the rest of the family are wanting to relax and enjoy a holiday or celebration, the person with ASD may become agitated by the break in routine. If a crisis arises, he will need a monumental amount of support at the very time when other family members are struggling themselves.

Families routinely provide support for an individual who may cause them pain. Inappropriate remarks can cause amusement if you are not involved, but the sibling relives the embarrassment of what happened in the local shop or in front of their friends. Parents cope with seeing their child's naive behaviour interpreted as rude, selfish or offensive. They deal with trying to protect them from rejection and bullying in the workplace or socially, whilst often feeling condemned by society because of their son or daughter's behaviour.

Living with John is living in a goldfish bowl. It is difficult being involved with professional support workers, especially ones who come into your home. Much as support is needed, it is a strain having outsiders around at all hours. Even when they are not there, conversations with friends and family are not private. John has no idea what is for public consumption and what is for intimate conversations only. When my mother was visiting, he told her that I had had difficulty food shopping for her stay, because she is so awkward about what she will eat. Fortunately, she knows that I love her dearly and the remark was made affectionately. On other occasions his repetitions have led to unfortunate misunderstandings. At home it should be all right to let off steam about the boss, to air frustrations and be free to joke about things. You certainly do not want such conversations repeated. I challenge you to imagine the effects of having things you have said at home or amongst friends repeated in the wrong place!

The hardest is going through all this whilst sometimes feeling there is no bond between yourself and your child. I saw a letter in a newspaper that describes how the writer has been saddened to read that a prospective adoptive mother, having decided to spend time in a nursery school to accustom herself to young children, finds 'that of all the children attending only one seemed difficult to love – and he had some form of autism'. I agree with the writer that, 'autistic children are most in need of our love and care', but can understand the woman's difficulty and appreciate her honesty.

Most children automatically know from a young age how to demonstrate their attachment – a smile, outstretched arms, a special look – unless that is, the child is autistic. John is unique; he is loveable and loving. I can laugh at his well-meaning, yet tactless comments, but it still hurts sometimes that there is not the common understanding and empathy usual between mother and child. The family suffer the immeasurable loss of never being able to have a typical relationship or conversation with their relative with ASD.

My son is now a tall, fit, good-looking young man. A remark most mothers would make with pride, but I live daily with the fear that his normal, attractive appearance will act to his detriment if he says or does the wrong thing in public. Any inappropriate remark or over-familiar approach to a stranger could lead to trouble. Along with many other families we dread the knock on the door to tell us our loved one has been attacked, in an accident or arrested.

The lack of recognition of the high levels of support needed for a person who may not immediately appear disabled, contributes to the fact that many families are struggling to survive with little or no external help. The effort involved in giving support is often not appreciated. John had 72 hours a week support, but there are 168 hours in a week. Many of the hours he was supported, I was at work. So I came home and did more than the work of two full-time care staff. Many would consider me fortunate in the number of hours' care we had, but unsurprisingly I was exhausted. There are numerous families who are stretched to the absolute limit. Parents are obviously getting older all the time and many worry about what will happen to their offspring when they can no longer support them.

The focus of this book is on how support can be delivered. This chapter is perhaps self-indulgent, but I think it has some important functions. First, for those close to someone with ASD: I find it useful to talk to and hear from others in similar situations. It helps me to know I am not alone with these problems, and so I hope reading this helps you. Second, for professionals, family are often a vital source of support for the individual. It is very difficult for anyone who has not experienced it to appreciate what life can be like for the family of those with ASD. It is crucial to have an awareness of this, and acknowledge that supporting the person should involve ensuring that there is care for the family too.

In short:

- Living with a person with ASD is stressful.
- Unpaid carers need support.

Working together

For many people the best solution may be a mix of professional and family support. The lack of availability of support and the difficulty in applying for it is only part of the explanation of why people with ASD receive little external help. Some families do not in fact ask for assistance, or have rejected

support. Many of the adults I speak to and/or their families have had experiences of dealing with professionals, who they felt had no understanding of
their needs, so have at best been ineffective and at worst have caused further
problems. Often support was not provided or broke down, because the
person did not find it met their requirements. Cooperative planning between
the individual, family and professionals from the outset will avoid such
problems and ensure effectiveness.

A knowledge of theories, general strategies and an impartial view are
advantages the professional contributes. It is important not to lose sight of
these underlying principles and aims, but also to realize that life is multifaceted and in reality there may be other variables to consider. Looking from the
outside, one sees only limited aspects of the whole reality of family life. I
recall, early in my teaching career, working with an intelligent 12-year-old
who was autistic. I was sold on the idea of encouraging the person to achieve
independence and give opportunities. I tried to encourage the mother to
allow him to run errands to the local shop. It was easily within his intellectual
capacity to remember, select and pay for a few items. I naively, arrogantly,
assumed that the mother was over-protective and did not understand the
benefits of fostering independence. She despairingly explained to me that he
could not manage this. She described how, despite his abilities, he would
take a slice of the cake she had made and not understand how she could
know he was the one who had taken it when they were the only people in the
house. I did not at the time understand what she was trying to say, but was
looking from my own narrow perspective as a teacher. It is fine to give
opportunities in the controlled environment of the school, but in the outside
world this mother's son was vulnerable to many random factors. He was vulnerable to teasing. If he picked something up and walked off with it, who
would understand that he did not realize the implications? His mother
appreciated the real-life dangers of her son going to the shop alone. The
family have detailed knowledge of the person with ASD, which are important data to be utilized in creating a workable, balanced programme.

In my professional roles in education, when I held a review meeting, I
would include the pupil or student and family throughout. I have learnt
much from other parents; I learn from students I work with and others I
come into contact with socially. People with ASD and those close to them
have a wealth of experience about the condition, but are often invited into
planning meetings only after the professionals have talked everything
through. Listening, and drawing on the expertise of those who have success-

fully supported the individual, whether or not they receive pay for it, has to be the most sensible and effective strategy in devising a support plan.

Consideration has to be given to the working conditions of all carers when putting together a support package. The demands of giving support can be high. In order for the person giving support to be able to remain alert and provide a high standard of care, his own needs for rest and relaxation have to be met. The hours of paid workers are naturally considered, but those expected of a family member may not only be long but also anti-social. Whilst my son had support workers for part of the day each day, I never had a complete day free, each day starting and ending with caring. This was tiring and there were few opportunities for social outings to provide a break. A full day out at the weekend was not possible and nights out usually ended with a ten o'clock curfew. When support is given collaboratively, there is co-dependency between the individual, professionals and family members. It is vital to all to ensure that demands are not made upon anyone in this network, which are unsustainable and have negative implications for health and well-being.

The person with ASD is the focus for support. This means that his views and ambition should be advocated by those giving support. This must be done with respect for the whole family. Advocating for a person is helping to put forward his views, but does not mean arguing that he should have whatever he wants. Families negotiate. The person has rights but must also live within this unit. Good support will assist the person to hear other's opinions and needs. Practical outcomes must be reached that suit all. The hours I cared for John were not in my working day. It would have been unfair to continually drag him to places he did not want to go, but I did have places that I needed or wanted to go to that he had to come to. Especially if the person is living with family, he must be expected to give and take.

The work of a professional giving support is not easy, and this is particularly true for those working with people with ASD. There are times when my son is endearing; when his good nature and his quirky comments are fun. There are others when he is repetitive, obstinate for no apparent reason and a pain. A person with ASD may be difficult to communicate with and appear rude or ungrateful. I hope that having read this chapter professionals will also realize how tough life is for family. It is all too easy to do as I did with the mother and see only a small part of the picture. This narrow perspective is demonstrated by support workers complaining that parents were going to leave their son with relatives during a school holiday and go away alone.

Their view was that they looked after him all term and then the parents were leaving him to someone else when it is was their turn. When the whole picture is considered the child is in school perhaps 35 out of the 168 hours in a week for a maximum of 40 weeks a year.

Those giving support professionally should have regular contact with a specialist who can support them and help them through difficulties. This person can also help to mediate between the differing needs of all involved. Professional support workers have set hours, the facility to phone in sick and a holiday allowance. No matter how tough their work is, the shift will end, and ultimately there is the option of leaving the job. Family members offering support generally enjoy none of these benefits. For staff embroiled in a demanding job, this overview may be lost and it is the role of management to facilitate cooperation, ensuring a balance is maintained with respect for all offering support and the stresses they face.

Continuous cooperation and collaboration are essential to ensure consistency and harmony. Wherever there is disagreement between family and professionals, I believe that the paid support should defer to the family unless there are proven, serious risks involved in doing so. As a professional, I would hope that the family agrees with what I consider the best course of action. If they do not I may hope to persuade them at some point, but for the present will support them in their wishes. As a parent I am torn in two whenever professionals follow a path that I consider is not in my son's best interests. I have the prospect of either supporting a plan that I think is unhelpful or harmful to my son, or of disagreeing with the professionals and leaving him hurt and confused in the middle of our argument. As a professional I know it is frustrating when the path chosen does not appear to me to be the optimum, but for the family member following a programme with which he disagrees can cause serious distress. Effective management is needed to deal with any differences of opinion between paid and unpaid support.

At times of crisis the strengths of all those giving support should be harnessed. It is my experience that families are often shunted aside and professionals are looked to for solutions. Enhanced professional help may be needed to handle a difficult situation, and to give increased support to both the individual and family. However, at any difficult time the familiar provides comfort and stability, and the loss of family support at this juncture is likely to exacerbate problems. The cooperation described throughout this chapter can only become more necessary now.

In short:

- Specialist planning is required from the outset to ensure professionals and family members support and collaborate with each other.

- The family has a wealth of experience and in-depth knowledge of the person, which, combined with professional expertise, creates the optimum benefits for all.

- Consideration should be given to the hours and conditions of family members offering support as well as those of professionals.

- Professional support workers need themselves to be supported.

- The wishes of the family should be respected, unless this would cause harm.

Case study 12.1: Darren

Darren's mother's account demonstrates the pressure that families can find themselves under. It tells the family's perspective on the difficulties experienced in finding support for their son, detailing their feelings of isolation, confusion and anxiety. It highlights how invaluable specialist support was in giving insight and enabling them to interact more effectively with their son, and their need for this to have been ongoing. Darren's support profile can be found in Appendix 1.

Darren *Darren is currently unemployed, and living by himself with the support of a homeless charity. This account is written by his mother.*

Our son, who is now 22 years old, was diagnosed with Asperger's when he was 17. Darren also has a rare chromosome combination which has affected his growth and development. He was always hard work as a child, in that we felt we could never get through to him. He seemed to have no logic and a very short concentration span. We questioned this with the doctor and were told, 'Oh, he is just a boy!' He never had any real friends, was bullied at school (we were told by school he would have to change) and hated new clothes, shoes or socks. All these things we now realize are characteristic of Asperger's. We carried on, just thinking we had a difficult child and that maybe that is the way boys are. Our daughter, who is 18 months older, was so completely different.

Things really became very difficult for us at around the time Darren was 16 years old. He walked out of sixth form college and, once the structure of school life had gone, things went from bad to worse. He became violent and aggressive within the household. At this time we were referred to a specialist, because of the problems with his growth. The chromosome problem was discovered and he was referred to a psychologist, because it was felt that the discovery of this disorder had an adverse effect on him, causing his behaviour to deteriorate further. This was when he was diagnosed with Asperger's.

The psychologist gave us support, helping us to understand the way he thinks and how to deal with him in a different way. She kept our heads above water and was the saviour who kept us going at times when we felt we just could not carry on. Even though our son no longer sees her, she volunteers in a social group which a few of us parents set up for these young people and adults. It started with a monthly meeting and was such a success it is now every two weeks; long may it continue!

In the past years, we as a family have been to hell and back. It became unbearable to be at home with our son, who was in and out of work (24 jobs in four years). He demanded money from us to enable him to drive round in his cars, which are the one obsession he has always had. He has little need for rest so his sleep patterns are erratic and he would be up and down all night, in and out of the house. Our daughter moved into an apartment with her fiancé, instead of waiting to save up for a house as they intended. We struggled on, becoming more and more exhausted, depressed and we realize now that all this was taking a heavy toll on our health. In September 2005, we had a major incident with our son and the police were called – not for the first time I hasten to add. We decided that this was the end of the road for us. We still loved our son, but could no longer cope. This was the worst thing we have ever had to do; we made our son homeless.

After spending the first night in a police cell, he slept nights in his car, before eventually going to a homeless hostel. This only came about through a contact with someone from the homeless charity, who attends our church. He told us that they have many young people, some with similar problems, who go to them. The support from the charity was, and still, is fantastic. Darren was allowed to stay for longer than the normal one month, as he was a special case. They helped him to find a flat and are still providing him with support.

Obviously things have improved for us at home, but our son is vulnerable and a constant cause of concern for us. He is managing in his flat with our support for practical matters, such as washing clothes, ironing and cooking meals, and the support of the homeless charity with sorting out problems such as bills. The main worries now are he still goes out in the middle of the night. So far only the police have stopped him, but it could be a gang next time. He has put a pan on the cooker, gone out to the shop, got talking to someone in the shop (he will talk to anyone) and forgotten about the pan. He has difficulty dealing with people and frequently says the wrong things. He has been attacked by a neighbour, who clearly has some problems of his own. These are just some of the things that have happened in the short time he has been on his own in the flat. They happened regularly at home of course, and these are the things that are on our mind all the time. We think of him as we get into bed at night and just hope he is all right. We limp along on a wing and a prayer.

There has to be more in life for our son than unemployment and being on benefits, unhappy, depressed, frustrated and with no future prospects. Darren is very intelligent and gifted. He has a very mechanical mind and is brilliant with technology such as computers, mobile phones and videos. He never reads any instructions, but just seems to know how they work. He is very good at art and design. He has a phenomenal memory for numbers; for example, after working in parts departments of garages and in a ceramic tile shop, years later he can still tell us product numbers and names and where they were in the warehouse! He would be a great asset to a business with the right understanding and support. We would love to see Darren have some sort of employment, where people were understanding, and living in a self-contained flat with support, so someone would be on hand (should he leave the pan on and go out) to make sure things ran smoothly and to plan a future for him to look forward to. We are grateful to the homeless charity that has helped, and continues to help, our son. It has given us our health and some sort of life back, but it is clearly not their responsibility. It is the responsibility of our public services, but unfortunately these young people do not 'fit in the box'. There are more and more people being diagnosed with Asperger's and some sort of service has to be set up – sooner rather than later.

◆ PART FOUR ◆

SUPPORT WITHIN SOCIETY

CHAPTER 13

Networks

Our personal support networks span out to include family, friends, colleagues and neighbours. We may accept or give practical help, such as child minding, offering a lift or lending something; support may take the form of a listening ear. Most people are helpful, and, despite some of the more harrowing reports in the media, most people seeing someone hurt or in trouble will try to assist. This can be anything from giving directions in the street to a person who is lost, to trying to help the victim of an accident. We also expect professional support at different life stages from services, such as education, health and social services. In the UK there is a legal requirement for these to offer special services to, or make appropriate adjustments for, people with disabilities. This supports the generally held view that they should be entitled to this, and most individuals would offer assistance to a disabled person in difficulty.

Social inabilities create problems for people with autism spectrum disorder (ASD) in establishing peer relationships and so naturally accessing the support that evolves between members of groups, such as work colleagues, fellow students or regulars in the pub. Asking for assistance appropriately will be challenging for people with ASD. Because they may not appear disabled, they are often not afforded the help that would be offered to a person with a visible disability. In practice it is often hard to make people aware that, although it is invisible, ASD is very real. A friend was distraught at receiving a visit from a benefits investigator following a complaint from someone that she was able-bodied and should not be entitled to benefits intended for disabled people. It holds true that 'seeing is believing' and many cannot understand how a disability can truly exist that has no outward signs. A student received much abuse from other students who could not see why he should be entitled to support services. This very intelligent, sensitive student said ruefully that he wished he could be in a wheelchair rather than have this disability. He would still be able to study and work, but he would also be able to join in normal social conversation, understand jokes and perhaps even find a girlfriend. The disability would be clear, and not a matter for dispute or ridicule. Many people with ASD find their disability compounded by those around them.

There is evidence that those with ASD also have difficulty accessing support from public services to which they should be entitled. My personal experience has been that we have had to fight for support for our son at every stage and that, of the support offered, only on the rarest of occasions has it been available from or under the supervision of a specialist. This is echoed by the stories I hear from people with ASD whom I have met professionally or socially. Parents have had to fight for provision throughout their child's schooling, and many accept that the only option when he reaches adulthood is to provide support themselves. The information in the NAS report 'A Place in Society' (NAS 2004) reveals a stark lack of support for people with ASD in the UK across the range of services. Their survey in 2001 found that only 53 per cent of those with ASD had the transition plan to which all were entitled in secondary school to prepare them for moving on to the next stage of their life. They note that adults often only appear on the services 'radar' when they reach crisis point. Forty-nine per cent of adults with ASD are still living with their parents. Although 70 per cent of parents felt that their son or daughter would be unable to live independently without support, 65 per cent of these adults had no community care assessment and are therefore unlikely to be known to the statutory agencies that should be supporting them. Only 6 per cent of adults with ASD are in full-time employment, despite their abilities, and the fact that many would be capable of work given support.

This section will consider measures for developing more practical support within society.

In short:

- We all rely on informal and formal support within the wider society.

- People with ASD have difficulty accessing support informally and from public services.

CHAPTER 14

Disclosure

It is not always possible to tell from meeting a person or even from having regular contact with him that he has autism spectrum disorder (ASD). Individuals therefore face the decision as to whether or not to disclose that they have the disorder. Having the condition acknowledged is an essential precursor to accessing support and being entitled to ask that reasonable adjustments are made for this disability. However, despite legislation, some adults worry that admitting to a disability is detrimental to their prospects in any situation.

A major fear expressed by adults I meet is that they will be seen as odd and different if they tell. Matt (see Case study 2.1) simply wanted to attend university and have friends like any other young man. To begin by telling other students that he had a disability would be to immediately set up a barrier in the already tricky arena of social relationships. Able people with ASD are only too aware that they are different and disclosure can appear to make the divide more concrete and vast.

The difficulty of not disclosing is that difficulties and anomalies are likely to become apparent. Using all the knowledge and coping strategies he can muster, the person with ASD is still going to meet problems and be perceived as different. Without disclosure, others can be perplexed by their behaviour. For John and many of his friends this will lead to them being teased and bullied. The advantage of disclosure is that it may enable others to learn which aspects of the person's behaviour are related to the disorder. For example, work colleagues can learn that the person is not purposely ignoring them when they speak, but is engrossed and has genuinely not heard. This understanding removes causes for friction and promotes cooperative relationships.

Fear of disclosure is often fuelled by the expectation or experience of others not understanding the nature of the condition. When I discuss this as a professional, people say they are happy to tell me as they do not have to explain, whereas they worry about telling colleagues or friends. Many people with ASD are themselves struggling to know what it means to them. They may have had a late diagnosis, or be coming to terms with how it affects them in a new life phase. With this uncertainty themselves, they are naturally wary of making others aware of the condition.

Generally disclosure is on a sliding scale. Most people tell close family; whilst it would probably be inappropriate to tell a casual stranger. Some will disclose to professionals, but prefer to keep the information from social contacts. For example, a student may seek support from teaching staff within the college, but not want fellow students to know he has ASD. Sarah was happy to discuss her difficulties with her manager, but did not want her co-workers to be aware. There are no easy answers as to who and when to tell. Disclosure to professionals in formal situations appears advisable so that all are aware of the condition and any differences are accepted and planned for. Informal social situations are more fluid and difficult to read.

When the decision is made to tell, it is a good idea to have some written information about ASD. This relieves some of the pressure to explain and gives the person something he can reread and return to with any questions. It may be useful too to have someone else present who knows about ASD and the individual. This again relieves some pressure, and, as friends with ASD will be the first to say their communications skills are not the greatest, it is good to have someone to help out. In formal situations the person chosen may be a professional, who can provide practical information about the implications in that environment. In informal ones it may be a friend, who can maintain the perspective that first and foremost the discussion is about the person and is a valued acquaintance. ASD is one part of someone's make-up and disclosure is an act of trust, to enhance the relationship by giving the other person insight into why he may say or do things in an unusual manner.

As a society, to promote support for people with ASD we need to create environments where people feel secure in the knowledge that disclosure will meet with understanding of the condition.

In short:

- People have fears about disclosing that they have ASD.

- Disclosure has advantages in enabling access to support and promoting understanding about differences from the norm in a person's behaviour.

- Disclosure is on a sliding scale, with decisions needed about who and when to tell.

- When telling, it is a good idea to have written information and/or someone to help explain what ASD means.

CHAPTER 15

Education

An integrated society

The foundations for support within the wider community must be built from childhood. This is a two-way process – the child with ASD needs to be supported to work towards adult life in society, and also relies on others being educated to be aware of autism spectrum disorder (ASD).

Mainstream school, with large numbers of pupils, much noise and other factors contributing to sensory overload, is not an ideal environment for those with ASD; however, it is possible to make adjustments for individual needs. Some parents opt for special schools in order to benefit from smaller groups and higher levels of support. Most such schools are for pupils with general learning difficulties, so offer a restricted low-level curriculum, and staff do not necessarily having training or experience of ASD. People with ASD report suffering a high level of bullying in school, and this is often cited as a reason for choosing the more sheltered special education environment. The overwhelming argument for attending mainstream is that segregation does not happen outside this setting. The child will still mix with others in the local neighbourhood, in shops, the park and so on, which may be harder if they have been segregated at school. Once they reach adulthood there are few sheltered environments, and many people are picked on at work or out in the community. Promoting an awareness of the nature of the disability and encouraging integration from a young age should cultivate more understanding.

Some youngsters in the final year at the school my son attended stopped me in the street and asked about him. They had volunteered at Barnardo's summer project, and been surprised to see him there. They had seen him being made fun of by other pupils, but had been unsure what was happening.

They could see he was distressed at times, but were perplexed by his 'silly' behaviour. Once they knew something about his disabilities, they always spoke to him, accepted his differences and afforded him some protection. The school had turned down my request to talk to pupils about ASD, feeling this would single children out as being different. However, having information allows members of the peer group to make informed decisions. Most people are not unkind, but are unthinking or, because of lack of knowledge about disability, make incorrect assumptions. Information is the keystone to promoting understanding so that people with ASD are supported by and play a full part in society.

Schools have a duty to promote disability awareness, but like many organizations they focus on the more obvious and visible. In the UK the Disability Discrimination Act (1995) puts a duty upon them to make 'reasonable adjustments' for those with disability. This can only happen if the staff have an awareness of disability and recourse to specialist support. A teacher cannot be expected to have the expertise to offer the support needed across the range of disabilities. The special educational needs coordinator will not have in-depth knowledge of all needs, but will liaise with specialists from services such as Reading and Language, Sensory Impairment and Behavioural Support. Unfortunately, there is rarely a service for ASD. Without this, teachers are unable to provide adequately for the pupil, and are also unable to educate other pupils about the disability.

A teacher is likely to be as baffled by the anomalies of the condition as anyone else. Teachers are often at a loss to understand why a child will persist with behaviour which results in being bullied. Without specialist training it is difficult to comprehend the inability to learn from experience or to transfer behaviour. It is incomprehensible that an academically able pupil cannot follow a simple instruction. The child will present the teacher with difficulties and so increase his workload. Teachers will need training, support and time allocated to learn about and work with the pupil. They play a crucial role in shaping young people's attitudes and so it is vital that they have access to the expertise to promote equality of opportunity for all.

Fortunately most people can transfer what they learn, and so what is understood by the experience of being with a person with ASD, comes into play when they encounter another person displaying unusual behaviour. Some people describe themselves as disabled by society, and for some with ASD society creates the problem for which it then condemns them. For example, pupils on the school bus would encourage my son to get up and perform one of the latest pop songs. Parents complained that John was endangering their children by distracting the driver and asked to have him excluded from the bus. He clearly needed to learn that this behaviour was unacceptable and could have caused an accident. He also needed reinforcement that he must consider why others are asking him to act in a particular way instead of following their lead. However, this dangerous situation was created by the interaction between *all* involved. We all depend on others to act responsibly, and this is doubly true for the person with ASD, who may be less able to recognize danger himself. Parents and teachers were offered an ideal opportunity to educate the other youngsters about their social responsibility. The neurotypical (NT) pupils would have less difficulty than John in assimilating this learning. The knowledge they gained might then be adapted to other similar situations, so that it would assist them in avoiding risk to themselves and others in future.

Education about ASD requires direct teaching, but the best teacher of all is experience. Adaptations are necessary so that children with ASD attend school with their peers. Children need opportunities to grow up together, so that they know the person not the disability. Youngsters who have grown up with my son and people who have seen him grow up are not thrown when he makes an odd comment or acts in an unusual manner. They relate to him, and ASD is a part of his make-up. An acceptance of the person gives a realistic perspective of differences. It is not that people necessarily develop strange behaviours; in some cases they do not grow out of childhood innocence. Education is the key to appreciating the many positive qualities of people with ASD and learning to accept difference.

Supporting people with ASD from childhood within the community is the cornerstone to creating successful integration in all aspects of life. It enhances mutual understanding, providing opportunities for those with ASD to achieve their potential, to the advantage of all.

In short:

- Education builds the base for support within the community.
- Teachers need training, support and time to fulfil this role.
- Education about ASD decreases misunderstanding and difficulty.
- Direct teaching is needed.
- Adjustments are needed in schools so that pupils with ASD are integrated with their peers.

Opportunities in further and higher education

People with ASD have many qualities which make them excellent students, notably their tendency to focus completely on the subject they choose, meaning they are enthusiastic and hard-working. Their unique way of thinking offers a fresh perspective and can introduce exciting new ideas. ASD does however create problems which may or may not relate directly to studies. Students will need access to support to develop their talents.

The UK Special Educational Needs and Disability Act 2001 (SENDA) places a duty on schools, colleges and universities to make reasonable adjustments to ensure that people are not disadvantaged because of their disability. Due to the complex needs of the person with ASD this is very difficult to implement in practice. Life in an educational establishment can pose a range of problems. There are the practical difficulties that most are large campuses, requiring the student to be able to find his way around the site, to follow a timetable and to cope with large numbers of other students and staff. For full-time students they may be away from home for the first time, and this major life change will be even more traumatic for a person with ASD than it is for all. Having to manage a new lifestyle and to organize studies is daunting. All the difficulties related to communication and social skills will persist, no matter what academic level the person is at, and may be more pronounced in this new environment. Academically the student with ASD may have problems because of difficulties with organization, understanding language and rigidity of thought. He may have good subject knowledge and skills but struggle to apply these to fit a particular methodology. Writing for a particular audience or taking into account other view points can be stumbling blocks. Frustratingly for tutors the student may struggle to change, and this can come across as not listening or being unwilling to take advice. Much college and university work now involves group work and making presentations. These present problems for the student with ASD, who is likely to find more traditional written assessments better demonstrate his abilities. Concessions may need to be offered regarding the form that assessment is to take. In examinations concessions may be needed to compensate for, for example, poor speed of language processing or problems with following instructions.

Students will need a review of support for living skills if they are moving away from home. They will need support with the practicalities of negotiating the campus and accessing facilities. They will need support to manage the stress of change. They will need support to develop a social life. They may need support with aspects of academic work. People of all abilities are affected by ASD, and will be studying at all levels.

Traditionally the Learning Support team within the establishment provides any extra support for students who experience learning difficulties or disabilities. These have mushroomed in recent years, as disabilities such as dyslexia and ASD are better diagnosed. At lower ability levels, the closure of day services and the drive to keep people in the mainstream have moved more people including those with ASD into the education system. Students with physical disabilities are mainly catered for through physical adaptations of buildings; hearing loops and British Sign Language (BSL) experts work with the hearing impaired; similarly, those with visual impairment are provided with specialist equipment and personal support; specialists should be on hand for students with general or specific learning difficulties, but there is rarely (if ever) support staff with training in the complex support needs of the person with ASD. Ideally there should be access to a professional specialist for advice even if other staff carry out day-to-day support. Advice about the best way to support will be available from the student and family, and this should be taken full advantage of.

Very able students may have ASD. The disability may be well hidden, but it is also very real. The first principle of offering support to such a person is to recognize the validity of this statement. Even if on the face of it the student has no problems, care should be taken to familiarize him with the campus, staff and systems. A regular appointment should be established to provide an opportunity to tackle any difficulties as soon as they arise. Careful listening is needed to establish the priorities in giving support. The student with ASD is likely to have a very different agenda to most. A concern should never be disregarded because it appears trivial. Support may be needed to organize academic work, but it may be needed for more practical help, to stop small matters developing into major stresses. There needs to be flexibility in the system to allow for this.

The more able student may be more aware of social difficulties, although still unable to steer his way through the social maze. He may be teased or ostracized by others, which he finds distressing, but be unable to understand how the situation arose or to rectify it. The student at any level needs the person offering support to be in their corner. It must be borne in mind at all times how difficult social interaction is for a person with ASD. The support worker, who is not a specialist, will need access to someone who can assist him to an understanding of the effects of the disability. This insight is needed to be able to advocate for the student as required to other students or tutors.

Valuing their many positive qualities makes working with students with ASD a rewarding experience. The big reward is, when the student says 'Thank you', it is truly meant.

In short:

- Students with ASD, including the very able, require support.

- Support may be needed in some aspects of academic work.

- Support may be needed to manage living skills and cope with stress.

- The student may need the support worker to act as an advocate with other students and staff.

CHAPTER 16

Employment

Finding work

NAS statistics show that only six per cent of people with autism spectrum disorder (ASD) (12% of those with Asperger Syndrome (AS)) in the UK are in full-time employment. This compares with 49 per cent of people with general disabilities who are employed. Anecdotal evidence tells of people repeatedly moving jobs, either because they are told they are unsuitable or because they are unable to manage. Given the talents which many with ASD have, this is a great loss to the workforce. For the individual, being unemployed adds to his problems. Rates of depression and suicide are higher than average amongst those out of work. Besides the advantage of an income, work gives a person a daily routine and a source of self-esteem and keeps him occupied. Being occupied, for a person with ASD, can be important in staving off obsessive thoughts and worries. Filling hours with a routine occupation creates a sound basis to build on. Meeting people at work can be a non-threatening social contact, and work is a starting point for conversations. Traits common to ASD, such as conscientiousness, attention to detail, perseverance and loyalty, are great assets to an employer.

Specialist support is beneficial to the person with ASD at all stages of choosing, applying for, beginning and maintaining employment. Career advice, tailored to the individual and therefore taking into account the effects of ASD, is vital. It is difficult for anyone to envisage what work in an industry or service is like until they have experience of it. These difficulties are compounded for the person with ASD, whilst, because of the problems with change, it is more important to try to make a good choice first time. Successful placements for people with ASD enhance prospects for others, whereas failures have the opposite effect making it more difficult for others to gain the confidence of employers. Having as much information as possible available to the person will increase the likelihood of making a suitable choice.

Career preferences are individual, as are the person's strengths and talents. As with anyone, the interests in a particular area of the individual with ASD must be matched to a job which utilizes his skills. He will be helped by a specialist who can ensure that he presents a rounded picture of his talents and needs to select an appropriate career, and who will clarify the work role to him. Consideration has to be given to areas where strengths can be best used, and to any particular problems that the person may encounter due to ASD. A visit to the workplace is useful to find out how he copes with the environment and to check for any sensory overload. The number of people sharing the workspace may be a factor. A minor adjustment in the surroundings can be crucial to success.

I hope a general raising of awareness about ASD will spill over into the workplace, but proactive measures are needed as well to encourage employers. The process of applying for work may be more daunting and difficult for the person than actually doing the job. Courses are run for people on how to seek work – and this is for neurotypical people (NTs). First there is knowing where to look for offers of employment, making an initial contact, knowing what to include on an application form and, one hopes, arranging an interview. Any or all of these can prove difficult – and then the whole operation has to be coordinated! Whilst the individual will need much support, employers can also be supported in making the way into work easier for the person with ASD.

The characteristics of the disorder mean that the individual may not make a good impression at interview. Social skills will not be a forté. Those offering support may be able to negotiate a more suitable form of assessment. Giving the person an opportunity to demonstrate their ability may be a more appropriate way to find if they are the candidate for the job. An interview is the traditional aid to a decision, but it is not necessarily the most effective method of finding how well the person can work. Mark, for example, whom we met in Case study 8.1, would find an interview difficult, but obtained his job via a work placement which gave the manager the opportunity to see him working. If there is to be an interview, the specialist can support by giving pointers to both interviewer and interviewee. The employer needs to be aware of any ASD traits the person displays, such as lack of eye contact. Questions may be prepared with support so that they elicit the information needed, but are specific, factual and clear. Broad questions, such as, 'Tell me about yourself', will leave the interviewee floundering.

A work placement is a good way to establish whether the person would be compatible with the job. This can allow him to sample it with no pressure on either employer or employee. It provides an opportunity to evaluate strengths, and to see whether it is possible to accommodate any difficulties. The placement can terminate at the agreed date, and the person will as a minimum have some experience to put on his CV. It may have highlighted a problem which had not been considered, and so give a pointer to a better option. Work placement gives the person a chance to demonstrate qualities, such as punctuality and perseverance, which only show up with time. Permanent employment can follow with both parties confident of success.

The route into employment is not simple, especially for those with ASD. However, there is an increasing recognition of the rights of people to work and a growth in agencies offering assistance. People with ASD have many talents to offer and there are great advantages to all in giving support to boost the percentage of them in work.

In short:

- Few people with ASD are employed despite their having much to offer.

- Interviews are not always the most appropriate way of assessing candidates, especially not those with ASD.

- Practical tests or work placement may offer a better chance to demonstrate skills and talents.

- Specialist support can assist both candidate and employer.

Keeping work

People with ASD tend to be loyal, to stick to routines and dislike change. Once they are settled in work they are conscientious and thorough, and yet I know many people have been unable to hold down work for more than a few weeks (or even days). Under the UK Disability Discrimination Act (1995), the employer should make reasonable adjustments for people with disabilities. Because of the complexities of ASD, specialist input is necessary to identify what is required. Whereas someone with a physical or sensory impairment is likely to be able to describe difficulties and will often know what adjustments they need, the person with ASD may be unable to pinpoint the problem, let alone suggest a solution.

Arranging induction for an employee with ASD can be an excellent exercise for any firm to improve their initial training for all staff. The person will need clear detailed instructions on all aspects of the organization and his duties. This will range from the general, such as a layout of the building, staff names and jobs, lunch times and refreshment facilities, to specifics about the individual's work. It is good practice for managers as they must ensure that instructions are clear, precise and unambiguous!

It is the infinitely varied, unstructured social interactions which cause many difficulties. A person, who has held his current job for over 20 years, tells of frequently losing work as a young man; one job lasted only days before the manager dismissed him because colleagues were uncomfortable working with him. He had no idea why this should have been. Body language that can be completely missed by someone with ASD may be very unsettling for colleagues. It is the unwritten rules, such as the variation between the manner of speaking to the manager and the tone and content of banter amongst peers, that will single out the person with ASD. Specialist support to observe and listen to the individual and his co-workers is useful to identify any problems in the early stages. As with any difficulty the sooner it is recognized and addressed the better. If it is left to run, the person's unpopularity will be established and attitudes will be hard to change. He will also have assimilated this behaviour and it will be more problematic to make alterations if these are called for. It may be possible to meet halfway with colleagues being more tolerant and the person with ASD making changes. Although, as previously described, rules and strategies are not foolproof, they can be used to assist the person to modify his behaviour, one hopes to the extent that it no longer disturbs others.

Disclosure of ASD, as previously discussed, is a matter for the individual. Where colleagues are aware of the disability, it can be described to them and they will have the opportunity to offer support. Realizing that poor eye contact, failure to respond to a question when the person is involved in a task, or making an over-familiar enquiry, are the result of the condition rather than rudeness or deliberate acts with an ulterior motive, can allow others to see beyond these.

People with ASD are generally physically able and fall within the whole range of mental abilities. These factors offer no explanation as to why the percentage in employment is so low. There are, however, some who would find the demands of full-time employment too taxing because of the extra effort required to tackle any task and the high stress levels involved. Unfortunately, part-time work is often not an option because of social security rules, which operate in such a way that those on low income are worse off than they would be on invalidity benefits. People may be classified as disabled and entitled to the relevant benefits, or they may be fit for work – there is no in-between. Whilst some people with ASD may be disabled by the condition they, and others, could benefit from their employment part time, yet this is often not a financially viable alternative. Voluntary work is an option for some; a minimal income may be disregarded as therapeutic earnings and does not affect the entitlement to benefits.

In the UK, government schemes are working generally to assist those with disability into the employment market and the NAS has set up Prospects, a specialist employment service designed for people with AS. However, there is a need for more specialist services to assist those with ASD in realizing personal ambitions and contributing to the workforce.

In short:

- Employers in the UK are required to make reasonable adjustments for people with ASD under the Disability Discrimination Act.

- Clear, detailed information at induction will assist all employees.

- Specialist expertise and early intervention can ease social difficulties.

- Part-time work would be beneficial for some if financially possible.

Case study 16.1: Emma

Emma values the support that she receives to assist her to work. Employment is very important in fostering her sense of identity and independence. Her story highlights again the inconsistencies in ability that typify ASD. Thus Emma is able to gain academic and professional qualifications, but needs support in the social and practical aspects of finding and sustaining employment. Emma's support profile can be found in Appendix 1.

Emma *Emma works part time in an office. She shares a house with her mother.*

Emma works for local government, and her job is mainly word processing. She is already well qualified, but is attending college to gain more advanced certificates in audio typing and Mail Merge. She is an intelligent, articulate woman. Having experienced other types of work, she is clear about what her preferences are. Emma is sensitive to noise. Initially she was directed towards child care and began work in school. Working with children, was as she says totally unsuitable, because she was unable to cope with the jumble of different voices and other loud noises. Emma far prefers to work with machinery than people. She enjoys her current work, but is concerned that it is a temporary post. She likes to be busy, to arrive and get stuck in to work, and she does not like to be interrupted when she is in the middle of a task. Emma feels that she has to be well qualified and work harder than others because of her AS. She has support from the Shaw Trust, a charity providing assistance to disabled people seeking employment. They have provided support both in her present employment, and in assisting her to find work.

Emma has a range of interests. She is fond of animals, particularly cats and horses. She sees these animals as having ASD traits. She enjoys horse riding, and is happy that there is a stables within walking distance of her home. She is keen to keep fit and attends the gym most mornings. She likes to go to the library, mainly to soak up the quiet, peaceful atmosphere. She is talented at drawing.

Despite her intelligence and skills, Emma struggles with household tasks, such as cooking a meal. Her mother has been giving her support, and Emma also uses cook books. Emma was unable to cross the road by herself until she was 17. The college were dubious about her ability and unwilling to admit her to its English course, but, when they did, she achieved A grades at GCSE for both English language and literature.

Emma is quiet, but once you are in conversation with her, you find she has a lively mind and a good sense of humour. She joked about a visit to the Science Museum and the effect of a display, which invited people to sample 'Unbearable noises' for people with ASD. She enjoys chatting, but feels there is a time and place for it, especially when at work. Emma very much enjoys attending the Tuesday Club, when she has a chance to socialize with like-minded people in a relaxed atmosphere. She participates happily in events organized by the club or her mother, but does not take the initiative herself to arrange to meet up with people or go places.

Emma is happy that she can work, as she enjoys the money and independence. She hates the idea of having to live on benefits, and also would dislike the difficulty of applying for these. She appreciates the support she has from the Shaw Trust, but believes that this should be provided as a right by the government rather than a charity.

Emma no longer has contact with her father. She is very close to her brother, who is extremely fond of her and provided financial support to enable Emma and her mother to move into their house. Unfortunately, he is unable to see them frequently as he and his family live about 200 miles away. Emma acknowledges that her mother gives her much help and support, and she would miss her a great deal if she had to live alone.

Emma is content with her life at present. In the longer term she would like to see people with ASD better represented in the media, especially on television. She feels that disability is too often viewed exclusively as people in wheelchairs. This is, she points out, only a small minority of disabled people. She would like to see people with ASD in popular programmes, such as soaps, so that the general public have a greater awareness and understanding of the condition.

CHAPTER 17

The Criminal Justice System

Victims of crime

People with autism spectrum disorder (ASD) are vulnerable to crime, because of their social naivety, lack of social awareness and inability to recognize dangerous situations. They are an easy target for anyone who tries to trick them. Their tendency to become totally engrossed in a task and lose track of what is around, leaves them prey to thieves who pick on the unwary. A friend became totally absorbed in a game on her mobile phone, forgetting that her purse was in an open jacket pocket. It was no longer there when she boarded her bus. This could happen to anyone, but ASD increases one's vulnerability. Once alerted to a risk the person may be fearful, but he will often be oblivious to the danger until it is pointed out. He may be unaware of the risks of being in a particular area or walking alone at night, and may not pick up on signs of danger that would be apparent to most. People with ASD are at risk of being attacked, simply because they behave oddly. Support workers should be proactive in engaging people in learning how to avoid situations and behaviour, which may lead to them being victims of crime.

Being a victim is distressing for anyone, but it is not difficult to imagine why it is even more confusing and disturbing for those with ASD. Like other personnel dealing with the public, police should have an awareness of and training in disability, including hidden disabilities. A checklist of the main indicators of ASD may be useful, but the disorder can be difficult to recognize immediately. Even an expert will need time to definitely identify it. It is a good idea for the person to have an identity card, which describes their disability and gives contact details for people who are familiar with the person to offer support. 'Autism alert' cards containing this information can be obtained from the NAS. They are available in several languages and also contain contact details of the NAS. Such a system, however, depends on the person or those around having the foresight to get this card. It then relies on the ability of the individual to remember to carry the card, to not lose it and to use it appropriately. Some people would find this difficult. From the individual's viewpoint, it might be simpler if there was a central register, so professionals were alerted to the person's disability as soon as their details were entered on a computer. There would of course be issues around data protection and the person's right to confidentiality. The individual would have to agree to being on the register, and have the right to withdraw. It is just a thought, that, in view of the complexity of recognizing ASD, this could be a supportive measure in ensuring that people have access to appropriate support in a difficult situation.

Professionals, such as police, would benefit from a simple list of the main ways that ASD may affect the person at a time of crisis. For example:

- The person's stress levels are likely to be exceptionally high.

- Sensory stimulation, such as noises, lights, even gentle touch, may increase distress.

- Disability in the area of social skills may make the person appear rude, hostile and possibly aggressive.

- Stress may produce odd behaviour in him, such as rocking, flapping or groaning.

- His recall of events may be poor, especially of time and sequence.

- The person may focus on an irrelevant detail.

- He may have difficulty answering questions.

It is important that the person has support from a familiar person and/or a specialist professional as quickly as possible. Other professionals can meanwhile be supportive by staying calm and finding an environment, which is as free from noise and other sensory stimulus as possible. The person should be allowed time and space to recover, and not restricted from using repetitive movements, such as flapping hands. Questions should be short using simple language, and the person will need time to respond.

Progress has been made in protecting vulnerable victims and witnesses giving evidence in court. Measures such as video links should be available to those with ASD. As when facing any traumatic situation, it is vital that an ASD specialist gives support. Victim support services recognize the need that many have for assistance, at the time of the incident, during the trial period and after. This is very essential for those with ASD.

In short:

- People with ASD are vulnerable to falling victim to crime.

- It would be helpful for police to have simple guidelines on how to deal with a person with ASD.

- It is advantageous to have a system which makes professionals aware of the individual's disability.

- A familiar person and/or a specialist in ASD should be contacted as soon as possible.

Arrest

Their rigid thinking and love of order means that people with ASD usually adhere strictly to rules and are by nature very law abiding. Unfortunately, rules are not always clear and social behaviour can be very confusing, so they are in danger of committing offences through lack of social ability, inhibition and understanding. Given the nature of the disability it is not surprising that people affected by it and organizations involved with it are concerned that those with ASD may fall foul of the Anti-Social Behaviour Act (2003). The term 'anti-social behaviour' means different things to different people, and even within the judicial system there is no clear definition. There is a very real fear that unusual behaviour which is not in itself harmful and has no malicious intent may be misinterpreted as being intentionally disruptive or threatening.

Those with ASD are very vulnerable to being misled by others. Naively hoping for friendship, they may follow the lead of others unaware of the consequences. They may take part in criminal dealings unaware of the implications of their action, both in terms of consequences and legality. People may simply think it is fun to encourage the person with ASD to act outrageously, without realizing that his lack of social skills may mean that he oversteps the boundary of what is acceptable or lawful. The absence of normal social skills and inhibitions can cause the person to act in a way offensive to others. The line between jovial bantering and offensive behaviour can be blurred. Sexual mores are infinitely subtle. Assault does not necessarily mean causing actual harm. Sexual remarks or a simple touch can be classed as a sex attack.

There are many instances where social ineptitude will result in problems. Looking at someone for too long, standing too close, asking an inappropriate question or sounding over-familiar are all behaviours that may be misinterpreted. They can be seen as aggressive and/or sexually inappropriate. Occasionally people with ASD react violently. This may be where they are teased or verbally or physically attacked for their odd behaviour and become afraid. Violence is usually a response to extreme anxiety or distress. The reaction may seem to most people out of all proportion to the trigger, but the agitation will be very real to the individual.

Strategies are needed to ensure that people are treated with respect and that adjustments are made for ASD. Normal police involvement has a high risk of causing escalation. The practicalities can be terrifying. Loud police sirens and flashing lights fuel sensory overload; touch may be painful; being taken to an unfamiliar environment and/or being restrained can cause real fear. In a stressful situation the individual's response may be abrupt, appearing rude or aggressive. Paradoxically his high regard for the police may lead, through the tension caused by finding himself in a situation so at odds with his understanding, to uncooperative behaviour. Anyone when scared enough may lash out and this instinctive reaction can quickly result in further charges. Alternatively the person may try to please or fulfil the role expected of him by creating information, which may lead to him making conflicting statements. He may even confess, to be helpful or to achieve a short-term goal such as being allowed to go home.

The person should be entitled to have an expert in the field present to ensure that the disability is catered for. Police need to be aware that:

- The person is likely to be experiencing extreme panic at the unfamiliarity of the situation.

- The person may be hyper-sensitive to sensory input: noise, lights, touch or smells. This may cause actual physical pain.

- The person may be unable to cope in a confined space.

- Unusual or aggressive behaviour is likely to be an involuntary reaction to these rather than hostility or resistance to the police.

- Verbal evidence cannot be relied on.

It is vital to contact a familiar person and an expert in ASD. A register of local experts could be held on a database, so that this could be arranged without delay. People with ASD are recognized as vulnerable and allowed an appropriate adult during interview. This does not offer parity with other groups. Because of the complex nature of ASD, the individual should be entitled to a specialist, who can interpret for him and advise other professionals about effects on communication, social skills and stress levels. An appropriate adult cannot be expected to have the expertise necessary to support a person with ASD, any more than he would be expected to have a knowledge of British Sign Language to be able to support a deaf person.

Police procedure is to question the person to ascertain whether he understands the charges and has the ability to know right from wrong. This discriminates against the person, who is at the stage to be verbally able to work out the correct behaviour, but completely unable to apply this knowledge. Many traits of ASD are liable to be misinterpreted by a non-specialist. For example, falling into speech patterns of those around can be seen as being manipulative and giving each person the answers they want to hear. In reality following speech patterns is simply a manifestation of the disability, whilst trying to give the person the answer he wants is a behaviour the individual learns in an attempt to fit in and be helpful. Explanations as to why the person committed the offence may be given by a professional, and he then tries to assist by passing this on. In one such instance a young man parroted the explanation given by the psychiatrist (which he could never have thought of himself), only to be immediately accused of excusing his own behaviour. The expert should be on hand to support, interpret and their evidence should be taken into account when referring the case for prosecution.

The person with ASD faces similar problems in court. He is likely to be in a state of high anxiety, which will exacerbate habitual communication and social difficulties. Even a person of high intelligence and with a good vocabulary will not process quickly what is happening. Their facial expression and tone of voice, as well as responses, will generate misunderstandings. My son smiles to show he is trying to be helpful. This may not come across as an appropriate response if he is being asked about an offence. He sometimes giggles uncontrollably when he cannot cope. Again this could be seen as very disrespectful rather than an involuntary reaction. The individual should have an ASD expert available to support him, and to advise the court of the effects of the disability.

I have been unable to find statistics for the number of people with ASD who are brought before the criminal justice system, but I have heard many tales of people sent to prison or mental hospitals. Research Autism are carrying out a study of those with ASD in a young offenders institute and a prison in the UK. If a court recognizes that the person has some mental or cognitive difficulty, the only option they have is detention in a secure mental unit. The premise is that the person either understood and was responsible for the offence and is therefore guilty, or did not and is therefore mentally ill and should be treated. A person with ASD fits neither category and both of these measures are counterproductive.

Sentencing should be a deterrent and prevent re-offending. It is unlikely that a person with ASD will be capable of seeing the direct link between his actions and the sentence, especially as court proceedings are slow and there will probably be a considerable time lag between the two. He may be incapable of modifying the behaviour even if aware of the link. In this circumstance, an awareness that certain behaviour may result in imprisonment increases confusion and stress levels, making the person more likely to re-offend.

A custodial sentence in prison or hospital aims to prevent further offences through education and therapy. For people with ASD, the affect of being removed to a strange environment is far more traumatic even than this would be for most of us. It is likely that little more can be achieved than to contain the effects of this. Conversely some find the routine of the place soothing, quickly becoming institutionalized and unable to cope with life outside. Keeping a person in a prison or secure mental unit is very costly, but the therapy a person with ASD receives there is unlikely to have any practical effect on subsequent behaviour because of his learning difficulties (these mean that the link is not made between theory and practice). The strain of imprisonment and the subsequent readjustment to life in society is likely to affect the person's mental health and cause further problems, possibly increasing the risk of re-offence.

A way of dealing with people with ASD is needed that is just, takes account of their disabilities, is a deterrent and reduces the risk of re-offending. This is a matter for judicial review. I can do nothing more than make suggestions from a practical point of view as to what would achieve these aims. The effect of the person's disability should be taken into account when referring the case to the Crown Prosecution Service. If prosecution is deemed necessary, it would be helpful to have the matter dealt with more speedily, as the person will have a poor sense of time and suffer disproportionate stress compared to the average person. This stress may result in further offending or disruptive behaviour, which may be problematic in itself and also will adversely affect the outcome of the trial for the initial offence. If the process is drawn out, the person may be unable to recall the offence and be too traumatized to understand the court proceedings. These factors put the person at a disadvantage due to his disability.

A person with ASD should have the right to an assessment by a specialist in the field. Currently reports are sought from a psychiatrist, who is an expert in mental illness not disability. Particularly when under stress, the person may show symptoms of mental illness, and there have been many cases of people with ASD being misdiagnosed as mentally ill. A specialist as previously stated should be a person with a level of professional qualification, who also has considerable experience of working with people with ASD within the community. The psychiatrist does not have this crucial knowledge of what is usual behaviour for a person with ASD. He is therefore unable to identify behaviour which was without criminal intent, but stemmed from the effects of the disability.

Sentencing should be decided in conjunction with the specialist on ASD. A level of punishment should be unpleasant enough to act as a deterrent, but not so stressful that it blots out everything else which includes the link to the offence. It is most important to take steps to control behaviour in the future. Some physical restraint or restriction on movement, such as being accompanied by a support worker at certain times or in certain places, might be necessary either in the short or long term. However, completely removing the person from his normal environment and having to reintroduce him to it is likely to increase rather than decrease risk. ASD is not a mental illness but a disability. There is no 'cure', but effective support can enable people to live safely and productively within society. Stress is often the trigger to anti-social or uncontrolled behaviour, so management is needed to reduce this. Specific education may be needed around the offending behaviour. Such a programme must be designed and implemented by someone with expertise in ASD.

The system does not currently make reasonable adjustments for disability when dealing with those with ASD. This results in inequitable treatment and increases the likelihood of further offences. This is an area that urgently needs studying to prevent crime and the consequent suffering, to the victim, perpetrator and families of each.

In short:

- People with ASD are generally very law abiding.

- People with ASD may commit offences due to lack of inhibitions, understanding and social skills.

- Police should be trained in disability awareness.

- A person with ASD who is arrested should have access to specialist ASD support.

- The specialist should interpret and advise at all stages.

- There is a need for review to ensure that people with ASD are treated fairly, and to ensure that sentencing does not increase the risk of re-offending.

Case study 17.1: John

My son John's level of disability makes him highly dependent on support. His life story demonstrates the difference that the effectiveness of support makes to him and those around him, and the wider implications for society.

John   *This is an account of my son, who is now 25 years old.*

Our son, John, joined our family when he was five. A bundle of energy, he careered up and down the three flights of stairs in our terraced house. The social work volunteer, who came to help me walk him to school with his seven- and eight-year-old sisters and our youngest in the buggy, ended up taking over the three girls, whilst I dragged John, who was yelling his favourite swear words. He had a fascination for electrical equipment, water and anything messy. He had no respect for anyone else's property – or person. He possessed an incredible set of lungs and could scream for hours on end. He did have an appealing smile, would chat to anyone and, worryingly, would happily leap into anyone's car given half the chance. He loved music, sweets and swings.

John was ill with meningitis as a baby and his development was generally delayed. When he came to us he was still in nappies at night, did not speak in sentences and his coordination was poor. He attended a school for children with severe learning difficulties. His previous foster family had teenage children, and at home he was passed from lap to lap. His foster mother commented that he would always be a child.

We worked on the knowledge that inevitably John would grow up and we had to prepare him for this. Initially steps were needed to calm his behaviour so that he did not totally disrupt the household. Our children had grown up with routine, something that I am grateful to my mother for teaching me. Meal times and bed times were orderly, and looking back this was helpful to John. He soon slept through the night and discarded the nappies. I now began to target behaviours that had to change for survival – his and ours. Initially progress was painfully slow, but we chipped away, explaining repeatedly and rewarding small improvements. Communications were kept short, clear and simple, and explanations always given. John began to enjoy the benefits of being with children his own age. He enjoyed going to the park, friends' houses and trips out. Soon we could take him on any of these with no worries. He moved to a school for children with moderate learning difficulties and later, at our request, he joined the girls in mainstream school with support. He happily played alongside other children, but made no close friends.

When he was eight we moved and the children changed school. They spent a term at home whilst we battled to obtain support for John in a primary school which could take them all. At home John needed far more support than the girls. Any inappropriate behaviour had to be dealt with quickly and clearly. There was no room to negotiate: he lived in a world of black and white, where behaviour had to elicit an immediate, consistent response or it could quickly escalate out of control. He needed reminders of appropriate behaviour and extra supervision in high-risk situations. Given these boundaries, he coped well; reminders were needed less frequently and people often commented on how well behaved all four children were.

John developed a good rapport with the head teacher and, in the supportive primary school, he blossomed. He was happy, and made gradual progress academically and socially. Following a timetable and moving around a large secondary school proved more difficult. Maintaining communications and consistency of approach was not easy with so many subject teachers involved. His biggest problem, however, was outside the classroom, where he was bullied. Eventually he was excluded and spent the last few months at a school for pupils with moderate learning difficulties.

We decided in the light of this experience that, rather than go to the local college as intended, we would look at those that specialized in providing for students with learning difficulties. He attended a residential Mencap college, where he could safely socialize on campus, and studied life and vocational skills.

The plan was that afterwards John would move into a shared house where there was round-the-clock support. This seemed a good time to move on, now that he was used to being away from home for several weeks at a time. The rest of the family was under considerable strain, especially as one of our daughters was seriously ill. There were various delays and it was almost a year before he moved into a house with two other young men. My relief at no longer having to provide his care whilst worrying about my daughter quickly turned to alarm.

John had all the skills necessary for independent living but needed support to organize his daily life. He had grown into a tall, handsome young man with no immediately obvious disability. His greatest interest was popular music, and he supported Manchester United. Given the appropriate support, he was capable of running his home, doing some work and/or study and socializing. He was friendly, polite and cooperated well with those working with him. The support, however, was so badly coordinated that at one point the support worker rang to warn me there would be no one to take over when she finished her shift. There was no routine or controls, and there was conflict between the social worker and the care staff. I was attending meetings with Social Services to look into how to rectify this, but after only a few months in the house John wandered off and was picked up by the police.

A nightmare followed. John had never had any of the aggressive outbursts that some people have. He needed support, but was always cooperative. He was likeable and very fond of his family. Over the next weeks he was shunted between different homes, hospitals and a young offenders unit. As he became more terrified, he committed further offences, including threatening a policeman. Despite all the tumult, he never physically harmed anyone.

However, he spent the next two years in a secure mental hospital 250 miles from home, where he was physically and sexually assaulted by other patients. The police took no action, and the only response we had to complaints to the NHS was that they had been investigated and upheld.

When he was released, we were assured that Social Services had a better support team to care for him. The plan was that I would live with John with staff providing support, whilst I worked and had some free time, so that they could see what the family did that was successful. Six months later John was to move to a purpose-built flat with the staff supporting full time. We were upset by the regression in John's social skills during his stay in hospital, but he steadily recovered. Individual staff supporting him had strengths, but there was no consistency, no detailed, structured care plan with aims and controls and no expert in ASD involved.

John became very settled in his house. He worked part time, attended college and did the household chores. He had a good social life with family and made friends of his own, mainly at the social club we set up as a voluntary group. It was almost two years before the flat was ready, and I was shocked when I finally saw it. It had a small living room that also contained the kitchen. I could not believe that anyone could design a flat for a person with ASD in which they would be exposed to all the sensory overload of a kitchen in a confined living area. I went home and cried.

I was physically exhausted from long hours of support on top of going to work. John was increasingly unhappy with the support he had from the agency. I was in the extremely awkward situation of either supporting him in his complaints, which would create conflict with staff, or dismissing his complaints and ignoring problems. For months I felt I walked a tightrope between not alienating staff whilst supporting my son. After the visit to the flat I posed the question to him, 'Where do you want to live, in the flat or this house?' His answer was unwaveringly the house. When I thought of the effect that moving to the flat was likely to have, I knew that there could be no compromise on this issue. I had to back him in his wish to stay in the house, that after two years he regarded as home.

The social worker talked at length to him, and agreed that it was in his best interests to stay in the house. Although this was agreed, John was very anxious that the care team could and would force him to move. Family and friends did their best to reassure him that this was not the case, but his anxiety was taking a toll on his health, which added to the stress and so fuelled the cycle.

The pattern throughout my son's life is clear: with appropriate support he is likeable and gets on with his life; with support that is poorly managed and does not understand ASD, he becomes depressed and behaves inappropriately.

He is currently in a secure mental unit. Security is strict, although he has never been physically violent and hurt or used force against anyone. He has little understanding of his 'offence'. If he were not disabled and did fully understand, it is doubtful that he would have been locked up at all, and certainly not for this length of time. He is becoming depressed at being away from family and friends. The cost to the taxpayer of not giving him the support he needed is upwards of £13,000 a month. The cost to him and his family is incalculable.

CHAPTER 18

Accessing Services and Benefits

In recent years there have been many improvements to allow people with disabilities access to facilities, and increasing opportunities in all areas of life. However, the process has in practice largely bypassed those with autism spectrum disorder (ASD). The disability remains shrouded by the cloak of invisibility, and when it is glimpsed it is seldom understood. Over 60 years on from when Kanner and Asperger first described autism and Asperger Syndrome (AS), there are still few services to support those with ASD. Improved knowledge of and provision for those with ASD, so that it does not severely handicap the person, is developing slowly.

Technological advances have brought major benefits in overcoming the negative effects of physical and sensory disability. For some surgery can restore sight or hearing. In other instances technology provides lenses and hearing aids to diminish the handicapping effect of disability. Technology allows even the severely disabled to have some mobility and means of communication. The wheelchair is the widely recognized symbol for disabled facilities. It is a clear, obvious support that allows the person access to many amenities. On the other hand, like the disability itself, the support required for ASD is invisible. A friend who works in a nursery described a visit by an education official to assess an autistic boy in their care. She skilfully supported the child, giving planned routine warnings that the play session was coming to an end and then giving clear instructions as to which toy to put where. The assessor did not recognize the support that was enabling the child to benefit from the nursery education, and was going to report back that he had no difficulty. The worker moved away from the child and gave him the same instruction as the other children had to clear away and move to the tables. Instead he hurtled round the room scattering toys and throwing chairs. Many adults, together with those around them, have developed ways of coping with the disabling effects of ASD which are not obvious to others. Support for a person with ASD is invisible, but its effect can be as profound as that of a wheelchair is to a person who is paralysed.

When my son is with family or other people who know him well, he will appear to have little disability. The support is like an iceberg, and the huge foundation of discussion and planning, the building of understanding and trust, means that only the merest tip may be apparent. I automatically scan for risks, word something in a particular way, give a recognized prompt to control a behaviour, move to a quieter area or suggest we leave as the venue becomes crowded. Adults with ASD and their families have developed high levels of expertise.

Support is difficult to access because of the invisibility of both the disability and the support. ASD often does not appear on forms that give access to support or benefits. Whilst there will be tick boxes for physical, sensory and learning impairments and increasingly for mental health issues, there will be no space for this hidden disability. At college, students and I found that there was no provision for this in the section relating to support needs. Academically able degree-level students were unhappy with the suggestion that they tick learning disability, nor was the idea of ticking mental health problems seen as an appropriate or appealing option. Support can be missed out on, simply because a box is missing on a form.

Any reference to ASD is conspicuously absent on forms asking for details of disability in order to claim benefits. I go all through ticking the boxes for my son and they reveal no difficulty. Yes, he can walk any distance, feed himself, wash, dress and so on. There are no boxes that deal with social difficulty and communication section seems only concerned with the mechanics. I am left trying on a sheet of A4 to explain a disability that causes controversy and baffles experts. It is the experience of many that they are refused benefit or support on the basis of a written form, despite it being apparent to those who know them that this is needed.

A definition given by the Autism Society of America says:

Autism is a severe lifelong developmental disability that typically appears during the first three years of life. Autism interferes with the normal development of the brain in areas which control:

- verbal and non-verbal communication

- social interaction

- sensory development.

This definition states the nature of the condition, but in practice ASD is often defined by its effects on the person's behaviour and not what it is. The result is that if the person no longer displays those behaviours, the disability is seen as no longer existing. Where someone is receiving good support, which gives him the ability to cope, then like the little boy in nursery he is seen as having no disability.

In order to ensure that people with ASD have parity with those with other disabilities and receive necessary support, the diagnosis needs to form the basis for an assessment for benefits and services. It follows that a person who is physically unable to walk needs a wheelchair; equally it follows that a person who has ASD requires specialist support. The physically disabled person does not have to repeatedly fall over in order to receive support, but to get support or benefits because of ASD it is generally necessary to display its effects. Assessors will ask about difficulties and how frequently they occur. The fact may be that problems do not arise, or happen only infrequently, if the person receives support. This type of assessment means that people with ASD who are well supported by family have difficulty gaining external support. It is a worry for families, who carry out this role efficiently, that the individual does not display symptoms that would bring services. As they age, parents' worry increases as they know that the person will not cope without support. The loss of support when it does come will be due to trauma such as incapacity or the death of the parent: the person has to deal with the trauma on top of the loss of support. This may be a rapid change and, even if it was expected by the people around him, may come as a total shock to an individual with ASD. Professional support given before parents become unable to carry on allows the support workers to learn and maintain good practices used by the family. They will have the knowledge and structure in place to continue with support and to assist the individual to cope with loss. Good support for ASD is unobtrusive. It is apparent only in the decrease in or absence of difficulties. The condition is, however, as the definition states, 'a lifelong disability'. It may be well managed by the individual and those around him, but it will not cease to exist.

It is estimated that there are over half a million people with ASD in the UK, but there are few ASD-specific services. Appendix 1 contains support profiles for those who took part in the case studies. They show a high dependency on family support, with support from voluntary organizations and charities such as the Tuesday Club, the Shaw Trust and the Charity for the Homeless playing an important role. Professional support is in the main offered by educational establishments or Social Services, rather than a dedicated ASD service or specialist.

There are examples of good support. However, to make it more effective and prevent people being overlooked or excluded, systems are needed to ensure that support is available to any person with a diagnosis and is assessed on the basis of this.

In short:

- Forms requesting details of disability, within any establishment, should include a space for ASD.

- Diagnosis of the disability should bring an entitlement to support.

- Effective support will reduce difficulties, but should not be misinterpreted as the ASD ceasing to exist.

◆ Part Five ◆

THE FUTURE

CHAPTER 19

A Vision
for Effective Support

I hope this book will contribute to the expertise that is being built among people with autism spectrum disorder (ASD), their families and caring professionals. Good support is built on sound knowledge of the affects of ASD. It addresses areas of difficulty and offers effective strategies to achieve the aims and aspirations of the individual.

My personal vision for the future outlined below is of a coordinated service for those with ASD that would ensure that people could readily access such support as and when they needed it. This support would be cost-efficient, because the rapid response and level of expertise would promote effective methods to deal with difficulties and pre-empt the development of more serious problems. This is my vision for a comprehensive, flexible choice of services to meet the needs of those with ASD. It would consist of the following.

Surgery

This would be a facility for people living independently, who need to see a specialist either regularly or on a drop-in basis. Some people with ASD manage with no ongoing support, but may need to consult a specialist quickly if they have a particular concern or a problem arises. A prompt, easily accessible service would prevent the build-up of stress, and the escalation of small difficulties into a major crisis. This back-up facility may be needed because of a particular life event, or simply because the person finds the normal stress associated with the condition, more difficult than usual to cope with at that time. It would be the equivalent to having access to a doctor who deals promptly catching a problem in the early stages, rather than leaving the situation to worsen for the individual, perhaps causing stress to other family members and with possible implications for others who come into contact. Such early intervention would not only prevent problems, but would also preclude the necessity for expensive treatment and so would be highly cost-effective.

For some, support may need to be ongoing. The difference between being able to manage or not will be, perhaps, a regular weekly appointment to talk through coping strategies, routines or problems. This support would assist the person with ASD in organizing and managing lifestyles, and monitoring and managing stress levels to pre-empt crises. There would need to be the flexibility to enable appointments to be more frequent at times when stress is increased. There would be the facility to provide, or to refer the person to, ASD specialists services in specific fields such as employment, relationships or leisure.

Outreach services

Outreach would be available to support projects, such as finding and attending a college course, or accessing employment. Besides working with the individual, this might take the form of working with others such as tutors, managers and peers. Some organizations, such as colleges, may have their own support workers, but they will not necessarily have expertise in ASD. The role of outreach may be as an advice service, to train in-house staff and act as consultants.

Outreach support may equally be required to help the person to manage leisure time and to accompany him to social venues.

Emergency support

This would be available if a person with ASD is involved with the emergency services or experiences any crisis. He would be offered an identity card giving details of contacts, including the emergency service number. A voluntary register might be useful so that medical facilities and other emergency services could access information online. There would be a specialist on call, who could give advice to the person with ASD and the professionals involved, and assess the support requirements.

Support in the home

Managing a home is a complex task, which people with ASD find difficult because of, say, the organizational skill, multi-tasking and variety of situations involved. The person may need support to facilitate this aspect of his life. The support worker's role would be to enable the person to manage the home effectively. This would involve planning with the person so that he or she could cope as independently as possible. It may mean being alongside as the person completes some tasks. It would never mean simply coming in and taking over household chores. Neither would it mean that the person supported would have to complete every task personally. It may be that the best way of the person managing the home is to employ a home help to do certain tasks. This should be discussed as part of the overall support plan, but respite from some tasks may enable the person to cope with all other areas of life.

Residential support

Some people with ASD would benefit from a residential setting. There has been a move away from institutional settings to providing support in people's own homes. This is a great move forward in integrating people within society. There are, however, disadvantages to the person with ASD in living alone. The first is that he may become isolated. Although having a need for some social contact, the person may find it difficult to initiate and so become increasingly lonely leading to further difficulties. The second is that support would be provided at certain agreed times. This may work for a person with physical support needs who requires someone to help at regular times with practical tasks, but the needs of a person with ASD are likely to be less predictable.

Many I have spoken to would like a type of sheltered accommodation, where each person has their own flat or house on a small complex with staff always on hand. They would like the privacy of their own space, which is very important to a person with ASD, and yet to have communal areas; to have the freedom to organize their own lives and yet receive support when it was needed. This type of accommodation would give the opportunity to socialize without having to make complicated arrangements. It would offer the establishing of a regular, familiar contact with other residents, without necessarily a degree of intensity that people can find a strain. Living in the same complex would provide a chance for brief meetings, which may satisfy the need for company without being over-taxing. The support worker would assist with the organization of activities, which tend to facilitate leisure. The aim of the residential complex would not be to segregate people with ASD, but to offer opportunities for them to support each other. It would offer a solid base, providing an opportunity to live securely in their own home and supporting them to grow in confidence so that they can better integrate into all aspects of mainstream society.

A support worker on site would give access to assistance as and when wanted. For some the necessary support may be mainly the reassurance that someone is there if needed. The support need may be little and often, such as a ten-minute chat morning and evening. The ASD perspective often drives the person to feel the need for assistance is urgent as soon as something troubles them, so that they will suffer disproportionate stress and precipitate further difficulties if there is not a prompt response. Support may actually be required infrequently, but when it is, it must be immediate. The most efficient way of providing such support would be to have small supported living units, such as those designed for elderly people.

High-level support

A minority of people with ASD, mainly those who have other additional disabilities, require a high level of support. By this I mean that they need constant supervision. It may also be the case that an individual needs this support at a particular period in his life: for example, the time when a person discovers his sexuality can put him at very high risk; the death of a parent or other important carer, or any other major trauma or change in lifestyle, may also mean that a high level of support is needed temporarily.

This need not be as intrusive as was necessary in the past thanks to modern technology; supervision does not have to be provided by a person being in the same room. Alarms could alert staff if a person leaves an area which is safe for him, or enters one which is not. For example, if the person manages in his home but is at risk in the community, there could be an alarm on the door to his flat. A residential set-up, as previously described, could be used with modifications and appropriate staffing levels.

The residents would benefit from the advantages described. Support workers would know all people in the complex and so there would be familiar staff there despite absences. Where a person with such high support needs lives alone in the community, one-to-one support has to be provided. This is a very expensive option and has many disadvantages. If the support worker does not arrive on time, the person is dependent on the previous worker waiting until assistance is available. Should the support worker be taken ill or suffer an accident, there is no other staff member on hand. There will be times when the person requires no active support, but will be, for example, watching TV, engrossed in an activity or asleep. These times will be monotonous for the worker, and the person receiving support is likely to find the presence of another person intrusive rather than supportive. It increases tension and is counterproductive. The support worker has to be highly self-motivated to work one-to-one with a person, and such work can be isolating and de-skilling. The person with ASD and his or her support will have to spend a great deal of time together, and this becomes very problematic when there is a clash of personalities between the two.

Support costs are reduced where people share housing, so that perhaps only one support worker is needed overnight. A shared house though depends on people being able to get along together. Given the social difficulties of people with ASD, this may not be the solution. Sheltered housing would give the individual their own space, whilst allowing support staff to offer a good cost-effective service.

Support groups

The ASD service would provide a facility to offer people opportunities to meet others in similar situations. It may offer the chance for groups to set up regular meetings and/or events to share experiences, ideas and to have fun. As a local group, of mainly people with social difficulties, their family members and a few professionals, we have set up a club which meets fortnightly. This provides a safe haven for those with ASD to socialize. It is a place where parents can chat freely about their son or daughter with no worries about being misunderstood, and even share a laugh about a situation which appeared dire when they were alone. Sharing information about success stories, how a particular problem has been dealt with or a worry all help.

Such groups could also invite speakers to look at aspects of ASD and hold discussions about topics relevant to members. It is an arena where role play could be used to help the development of social skills.

The social group should be seen, not only as a resource in itself, but also as a springboard from which it is hoped people will make friends, and continue to widen their social circle and participation in all aspects of society.

The aim for all support should be to facilitate people in living independently, safely and happily, with opportunities to fulfil their educational, vocational and social aspirations. A comprehensive service as I have described would fulfil this role in a cost-effective way.

In short, ideally a dedicated support service for those with ASD would exist to offer:

- A surgery to meet immediate, low-level needs.
- Specialist support which is immediately available in case of emergency.
- Home management services.
- Outreach provision within education, employment and to access social facilities.
- Supported housing.
- Support groups to offer opportunities for sharing and self-help.

CHAPTER 20

Conclusion

There are tales in Indian culture of men who encounter an elephant for the first time. These men are either blind or meet the animal at night so cannot see it. Each touches a different part and draws a different conclusion. For example, the man touching its leg concludes it is a pillar, another touching the ear decides it is a fan, another feeling the trunk assumes it resembles a hosepipe, yet another taking the tail concludes it is a stick and so on. None could form an accurate opinion of the whole by experiencing only one part. Each took his own knowledge and expressed it in terms of things already familiar to him.

Autism spectrum disorder (ASD) is a multifaceted difference from the average which is intricately woven into the make-up of an individual. Those who see only limited facets will have an unreal picture of the condition and of the person. I am aware that throughout this book I have presented a skewed view of the condition. The purpose of the book is to put forward practical ideas for support. In order to demonstrate the support needed it has been necessary to concentrate on the disabling features of the condition, and in some cases to describe the worst possible scenarios. I hope it achieves the aims of highlighting support needs and giving practical ideas for meeting them. However, anyone who wishes to know the complete nature of ASD must spend time with people who have the condition learning about all its qualities, and, as they observe and listen, be prepared to put aside all preconceptions to gain insight into this remarkable difference.

An understanding of ASD by society as a whole is essential to eradicating problems and discrimination faced by those who have it. In order for this to happen neurotypicals (NTs) need a full, rounded picture. There is a paradox in that ASD is all pervasive, affecting every aspect of a person's dealings, and yet it is also only one part of his make-up. It is like looking at something through coloured glass. The glass will affect everything seen but beyond that everything maintains it uniqueness and infinite variety. ASD 'colours' everything about the person, but it is a surface aspect and beyond it each person is his own unique, valuable self.

It is a 'Catch 22' situation in that it is difficult for the individual to disclose that he has ASD whilst there is ignorance and misunderstanding about the condition, and yet this will persist if others do not learn about it from people with ASD. Role models have been helpful in demonstrating that having a particular disability does not mean that is the person's defining quality, or a bar to achievement. Successful people such as the entrepreneur Richard Branson, the architect Richard Rogers and the actress Susan Hampshire have acknowledged that they are dyslexic. Such role models have done much to remove misunderstanding and the perceived stigma attached to dyslexia. Research demonstrates that many high achievers in all fields are likely to have had ASD. Michael Fitzgerald (2005) looks at famous people who he considers had the disorder, including Beethoven, George Orwell and Andy Warhol. The nature of ASD means that people who have it do not like to draw attention to themselves, but if successful people did disclose they would create role models that make it easier for others.

In order to manage and deal with the disabling aspects of ASD, it needs to be out in the open. Successful role models help, as discussed, and there is also a need for people with ASD to be portrayed and represented throughout the mainstream media. We need characters in popular TV programmes who have ASD; not stories about ASD, but a character say in a popular soap who just happens to have the condition (see Emma's comments in Case study 16.1).

Internationally, awareness is growing of the need to promote equality. Many countries have signed up to the UN Convention on the Rights of Persons with Disabilities which opened for signature on 30 March 2007. This places a responsibility on the state to protect the rights of all with disabilities, to provide services and to promote inclusion in education, employment and all areas of society. It requires it to ensure that:

> Persons with disabilities have access to a range of in-home, residential and other community support services, including personal assistance necessary to support living and inclusion in the community, and to prevent isolation or segregation from the community. (Article 19)

Although human rights systems were intended to promote and protect the rights of all, UN Human Rights Commissioner Louise Arbour states that 'the existing standards and mechanisms have in fact failed to provide adequate protection to the specific cases of persons with disabilities' (United Nations 2006). This convention aims to correct this deficiency. As awareness of disability is raised generally, I hope that well-designed and managed support will become widely available for those with hidden disabilities such as ASD.

Beyond the glass wall of ASD there are exceptional people. Good support keeps the glass clear so that those on both sides benefit; without it the world on the other side becomes darker and gloomier until, in some cases, it is so murky that the person blunders blindly and crashes.

As well as causing sadness for the individual and their family, society as a whole loses if it does not facilitate people with ASD to live well. If we invest wisely in constructive support assisting people to achieve their potential, there is much to gain for the individual and the community.

Appendix 1

Support Profile

Matt

Support history
- Learning advisor in sixth form.
- Learning advisor at university.

Present support needs	Support provided by	Outcome
Home Matt easily becomes worried and needs support to talk though any perceived problems.	Parents	Reassurance and support are readily available.
Study Matt benefits from support to organize work, interpret questions and deal with social issues.	Learning support tutor	Matt is in the final stage of completing his degree.

Comments
Matt has found his ASD restricted the choice of employment open to him to fund his study.

Projected support needs
Specialist support from an employment advisor would be useful as Matt finishes his studies.

Matt has an ongoing need for support with social issues and to talk through concerns.

Support Profile

Harry

Support history

- Advice from specialist doctor during childhood.
- Boarding school.
- Support from psychologist specializing in ASD following specific problems.

Present support needs	Support provided by	Outcome
Home Harry easily becomes worried by issues such as the breakdown of a domestic appliance or any unexpected event.	Family, particularly mother	Harry is able to talk through issues, which relieves stress.
Work Harry needs people at work to be understanding when he misreads social cues.	Employer	Harry's employer has previous experience of knowing someone with ASD and Harry feels he is understanding, although others in the workforce may be less knowledgeable.
Social Harry would like a more active social life. He lacks confidence in many social venues, as he is worried that misinterpretation of social cues may cause problems.	Tuesday Club	Harry meets people in the safe friendly environment of the club every two weeks. He has the opportunity to contribute to planning and take part in outings with the group.
	Family members, particularly children	Harry enjoys social venues in the company of family members.
	Church	Harry is a regular churchgoer and feels benefits as part of this community.

Comments

Harry feels his support needs are met currently.

Projected support needs

More support will be needed at home if Harry's mother becomes unable to support him.

Support Profile

Mark

Support history

- Support from Health Service pre-school due to developmental delay.
- Support for non-specific learning difficulties in mainstream primary.
- Secondary school for pupils with moderate learning difficulties.
- Support in college on course for students with disabilities.
- Support from employer on work placement and in subsequent employment.
- Aged 23, support from psychologist diagnosing ASD.

Present support needs	Support provided by	Outcome
Home Mark needs practical support with daily living skills and managing money.	Parents	Mark lives with his parents. All living and budgetary requirements are met.
Mark easily becomes anxious. He needs reassurance and support to deal with stress.	Parents mainly, and other family members	Mark has the support he needs to cope with daily living and full-time employment.
	Family doctor	Anti-depressants provide some relief.
Work Mark can cope with the practical aspects of his job. He is easily upset by any misunderstanding. He finds any change difficult to manage.	Employer	Mark works full time. His employer is supportive and understanding, but has no back-up from specialist service. The quality of daily support depends on staffing.
Social Mark would like a more active social life. He is shy, lacking in confidence and finds some social environments too noisy and confusing.	Tuesday Club	Mark meets people in the safe friendly environment of the club every two weeks. He has the opportunity to contribute to planning and take part in outings with the group.

Comments

Mark appreciates the support offered by his employer, but feels it would be beneficial to have some input from a specialist in ASD.

Mark's parents feel under strain, and this affects their health.

Projected support needs

Mark and his family recognize that he is at an age where most people live independently. They would like to plan for this and, as his parents age, professional support with living will become a necessity.

Support Profile

Emma

Support history

- School for pupils with special educational needs.

Present support needs	Support provided by	Outcome
Home Emma required guidance with domestic tasks: she can follow a recipe, but needs many repetitions to learn some tasks, for example frying an egg.	Mother	Emma prepares most of her own meals.
Work Emma can search for jobs, but needs support in applying for work.	Shaw Trust	Emma works part time. She is being assisted to apply for another post.
Emma is very competent in her work, but needs support in negotiating with colleagues.		
Social Emma enjoys social events, but needs support to initiate these.	Mother	Emma's mother provides company at home and arranges outings.
Emma finds some social environments too noisy and chaotic, so needs support to find suitable venues.	Tuesday Club	Emma meets people in the safe friendly environment of the club every two weeks. She has the opportunity to contribute to planning and take part in outings with the group.

Comments

Emma feels the support she receives meets her current needs, but is unhappy that support at work depends on a voluntary organization.

Projected support needs

Emma will need more professional support as her mother becomes older.

Support Profile

Darren

Support history

- Support from psychologist specializing in ASD, who made diagnosis.
- Advice and support for parents from psychologist.

Present support needs	Support provided by	Outcome
Home Darren needs support to organize daily living skills. He needs support with managing money.	Parents, homeless charity	Darren is living independently, although there are still concerns about his safety.
Social Darren becomes extremely depressed, sometimes as a result of an incident.	Parents	Darren's parents assist him with any practical crises. They provide support by talking through sources of depression.

Comments

Darren's current situation causes his family much concern. He is largely unsupported in his flat and there have been dangerous incidents, such as his going out and leaving a pan on the stove. Socially he puts himself in situations which generate risk.

He suffers from a lack of structure in his life, and requires support to find and sustain suitable employment.

He would benefit from a holistic assessment of his needs and a comprehensive support package.

Projected support needs

The support needs identified will continue.

Darren will need further professional support with living if the charity becomes unable to fund this.

Darren will need increased support with living skills as his parents become older.

Appendix 2

Project – Planning a weekend away	Week 1 w/c…	Week 2 w/c…	Week 3 w/c…	Week 4 w/c…	Week 5 w/c…	Week 6 w/c…	Week 7 w/c…
Research place of interest and select town	■						
Make list of suitable accommodation in the town		■					
Book accommodation. Book train or coach ticket.			■				
Write list of items to pack for trip. Buy any necessities.				■			
Relax!					■	■	
Thursday: pack case, check travel details Friday: travel							■

References

Autism Society of America (n.d.) 'Defining Autism.' Available at www.autism-society.org/site/PageServer?pagename=about_whatis_home, accessed on 25 January 2008.

Birch, J. (2003) *Congratulations! It's Asperger Syndrome.* London: Jessica Kingsley Publishers.

Fitzgerald, M. (2005) *The Genesis of Artistic Creativity.* London: Jessica Kingsley Publishers.

Grandin, T. (1995) *Thinking in Pictures.* New York: Vintage Books.

Holliday Willey, L. (1999) *Pretending to be Normal.* London: Jessica Kingsley Publishers.

Howard, R. (2001) *A Beautiful Mind.* Universal Pictures and Dreamworks.

McLoughlin, D., Leather, C. and Stringer, P. (2002) *The Adult Dyslexic.* London: John Wiley & Sons.

Morrell, M. and Palmer, A. (2006) *Parenting Across the Autism Spectrum.* London: Jessica Kingsley Publishers.

National Autistic Society (1999) 'Opening the door.' London: National Autistic Society.

National Autistic Society (2004) 'A Place in Society.' London: National Autistic Society.

United Nations (1996) 'General Assembly Ad Hoc Committee, 7th Session: Statement by Louise Arbour.' Available at www.un.org/esa/socdev/enable/rights/ahc7stathchr.htm, accessed on 25 January 2008.

Williams, D. (1992) *Nobody, Nowhere.* New York, NY: Times Books.

Williams, D. (1994) *Somebody, Somewhere.* London: Jessica Kingsley Publishers.

Further Reading

Baker, J. (2005) *Preparing for Life: The Complete Guide for Transitioning to Adulthood for Those with Autism and Asperger's Syndrome.* Arlington, TX: Future Horizons.

Barnard, J., Harvey, V., Prior, A. and Potter, D. (2000) *Inclusion and Autism: Is it Working?* London: National Autistic Society.

Fast, Y. (2004) *Employment for Individuals with Asperger Syndrome or Non-Verbal Learning Disability: Stories and Strategies.* London: Jessica Kingsley Publishers.

Grandin, T. and Barron, S. (2005) *The Unwritten Rules of Social Relationships: Decoding Social Mysteries Through the Unique Perspective of Autism.* Arlington, TX: Future Horizons.

Harpur, J., Lawlor, M. and Fitzgerald, M. (2004) *Succeeding in College with Asperger Syndrome.* London: Jessica Kingsley Publishers.

Howlin, P. (2004) *Autism and Asperger Syndrome: Preparing for Adulthood* (2nd ed.). London: Routledge.

Korin, E. (2006) *Asperger Syndrome: An Owner's Manual 2 For Older Adolescents and Adults: What You, Your Parents and Friends, and Your Employer, Need to Know.* Shawnee Mission, KS: Autism Asperger Publishing Company.

Lever, N. (2006) *The Transporters – Discover the World of Emotions.* Sydney: Doubleday. Online and Autism Research Centre, Cambridge.

Meyer, R. (2000) *Asperger Syndrome Employment Workbook: An Employment Workbook for Adults with Asperger Syndrome.* London: Jessica Kingsley Publishers.

Murray, D. (2006) *Coming Out Asperger: Diagnosis, Disclosure and Self-Confidence.* London: Jessica Kingsley Publishers.

National Autistic Society (2005) *Employing People with Asperger Syndrome: A Practical Guide.* London: NAS.

Notbohm, E. and Zysk, V. (2005) *Ten Things Your Student with Autism Wishes You Knew.* Arlington, TX: Future Horizons.

Pike, R. (2005) *Supporting Students with Asperger Syndrome in Higher Education.* London: National Autistic Society.

Smith, M., Belcher, R. and Juhrs, P. (1994) *A Guide to Successful Employment for Individuals with Autism.* Baltimore, MD: Paul H. Brookes.

Useful Organizations

A4 – Autism Aspergers Advocacy Australia
PO Box 717
Mawson, ACT 2607, Australia
Website: www.a4.org.au

Autism Asperger ACT
c/o SHOUT, PO Box 717
Mawson, ACT 2607, Australia
Telephone: +61 (0) 2 6290 1984
Website: www.assn.org.au

Autism New Zealand Inc.
Level 1, 257 Lincoln Road, Addington
Christchurch 8149, New Zealand
Telephone: +64 3332 2627
Website: www.autismnz.org.uk

Autism Research Institute
4182 Adams Avenue San Diego, CA 92116, USA
Telephone: +1 (866) 366 3361
Website: www.autism.com

Autism Society America (ASA)
7910 Woodmont Avenue, Suite 300
Bethesda, MD 20814 – 3067, USA
Telephone: +1 (301) 657 0881 or +1 (800) 3AUTISM (328 8476)
Website: www.autism-society.org

Autism Society Canada
Box 22017
1670 Heron Road
Ottawa, ON K1V 0C2, Canada
Telephone: +1 (613) 789 8943
Website: www.autismsocietycanada.ca

Autism Spectrum Australia (Aspect)
PO Box 361, 41 Cook Street

Forestville, NSW 2087, Australia
Telephone: +61 (0) 8977 8300
Website: www.aspect.org.au

Autism Treatment Services of Canada
Telephone: +1 (403) 253 6961
Website: www.autism.ca

Missing Link Support Services
(Consultant psychologist – E. Veronica (Vicky) Bliss)
Clarks Cottage, Union Lane
Out Rawcliffe PR3 6SS, UK
Telephone: 07971 569042
Webiste: www.missinglinksupportservice.co.uk

National Autism Association
1330 W. Schatz Lane
Nixa, MO 65714, USA
Telephone: +1 (877) NAA AUTISM (877 622 2884)
Website: www.nationalautismassociation.org

The National Autistic Society (NAS)
393 City Road
London EC1V 1NG, UK
Telephone: 020 7833 2299
Website: www.autism.org.uk

Research Autism
28 Blakesware Gardens
London N9 9HU, UK
Telephone: 020 8292 8900
Website: www.researchautism.net

An international index of societies supporting those with ASD is available at:
www.autismuk.com/index6.htm

Index

accessing services and benefits 164–7
accidents 41
accommodation
    Criminal Justice System 161–2, 163
    education 143
    family support 130, 131
    health 90, 93
    high-level support 175
    networks 136
    organization 44
    residential support 173
    support in the home 172–3
achievement 50, 51
ADHD (Attention Deficit Hyperactivity
    Disorder) 12
alcohol 79
anti-depressants 88
Anti-Social Behaviour Act (2003) 79,
    155
Arbour, Louise 179
arrest 155–60
AS see Asperger Syndrome
ASD see autism spectrum disorder
Asperger, Hans 11, 164
Asperger Syndrome (AS)
    accessing services and benefits 164
    definition of autism 11, 14
    employment 146, 150
    family support 129, 130, 131
    understanding the nature of ASD 22,
        26, 27, 28
assault 155
Attention Deficit Hyperactivity Disorder
    (ADHD) 12
attention span 50, 51
autism 11, 14, 22 see also autism
    spectrum disorder
'Autism alert' cards 153
Autism Society of America 165
autism spectrum disorder (ASD)
    accessing services and benefits 164,
        165, 166
    care plans 105
    communication
        case study 62
        clear communication 54, 55, 56
        difficulties 52, 53

listening 57, 58, 59, 60
more than words 64, 65
Criminal Justice System
    arrest 155, 156, 157, 158, 159
    victims of crime 153, 154
definition 11–4, 165, 177, 178, 179
disclosure 137, 138
education 140, 141, 142, 144
employment 146, 147, 148, 149,
    150, 152
ethics 119, 120
family support 123, 126, 127
health 84, 89, 90, 91, 94
interpretation 47, 48, 49, 50, 51
key areas for support 31, 32, 33, 34
managing support 101, 102, 103–4
networks 135, 136
organization
    forward planning 43, 44, 45, 46
    instilling order 35, 36, 37
    managing change 39, 40, 41, 42
prevalence 17
social interaction
    anti-social behaviour 80, 82
    coping strategies 72, 73
    difference 67, 68, 69, 70
    sex 74, 75, 76, 77, 78
support needs 17, 18, 19, 20, 21
understanding the nature of ASD
    22–8
useful organizations 188–9
vision for effective support 171,
    172, 173, 174, 175

A Beautiful Mind 76
Beethoven, Ludwig van 178
benefits 150, 151, 164–7
bereavement 41, 174
Birch, Jen 23
Blackburn, Ros 52
body language 149
boyfriends 74, 75 see also sex
Branson, Richard 178
British Sign Language (BSL) 144, 157
bullying
    care plans 107
    communication 62

disclosure 137
education 140, 141
family support 124
health 87, 88
social interaction 67, 70

career advice 59, 60, 146–7
care plans 105–18
    design 105–14
    implementation 114–18
case studies
    communication 61–3
    Criminal Justice System 160–3
    employment 150–2
    family support 129–31
    health 86–90
    understanding the nature of ASD
        26–8
change 39–42, 143
checklists 36, 115, 185
choice 44, 46
cleaning 115, 116
clubs 71, 72, 151, 166, 175–6
college
    accessing services and benefits 165
    communication 57
    Criminal Justice System 161
    education 143
    employment 151
    health 92
    key areas for support 32
    organization 40
    outreach services 172
communication 52–66
    care plans 115
    case study 61–3
    clear communication 54–6
    complexity 65–6
    definition of autism 11
    difficulties 52–4
    key areas for support 31, 32, 33
    listening 56–61
    more than words 63–5
    social interaction 67
    understanding the nature of ASD 23,
        24
communications book 115, 116

confidentiality 119, 154
connections 47–50
consent 76, 121
consequences 47, 48
contingency plans 41
conversations
    communication 52, 53, 56, 62, 64,
        65
    family support 124
    social interaction 67–8, 71
cooking 38, 90, 151
counselling 74–5
courts 154, 158, 159
Criminal Justice System 153–63
    arrest 155–60
    case study 160–3
    victims of crime 153–5
crisis points 41, 42
Crown Prosecution Service 158

decision-making process 43, 44, 45, 46
depression 34, 43, 90, 146, 163
diagnosis 22, 89, 138
diet
    care plans 110, 111, 115
    employment 151
    health 85
    key areas for support 32–3
    organization 37, 44
disability
    accessing services and benefits 164,
        165, 166
    anti-social behaviour 80
    communication 61
    Criminal Justice System 153, 154,
        156, 157, 158, 159
    definition of ASD 178, 179
    disclosure 137
    education 140, 141, 142, 143, 144
    employment 146, 148, 149, 150,
        151, 152
    family support 123
    key areas for support 33
    networks 135, 136
    support needs 19, 21
    understanding the nature of ASD 24,
        25
Disability Discrimination Act (1995)
    141, 148
disclosure 137–9, 149, 178
distance 73
distractions 50, 54, 56, 59
duty of care 119, 121
dyslexia 12, 19, 80, 144, 178

echolalia 53
education 140–5 see also college; school;
    university
emergency support 172
emotions 68, 69, 70
empathy 67, 91, 124
employment 146–52
    case study 150–2
    family support 131
    finding work 146–8

health 87, 88, 91–2
    interpretation 47, 48
    keeping work 148–50
    networks 136
    outreach services 172
environment 54, 59–60
ethics 119–21
examinations 143
exercise 94
explanations 47, 48, 49, 51
eye contact 63, 147, 149

facial expression 27, 54, 63, 157
family support 122–31
    caring for the family/carers 122–5
    case study 129–31
    support needs 18
    working together 125–9
fears 86, 87, 93
figurative language 58
finances 90, 96, 120, 151
Fitzgerald, Michael 178
food see diet
forward planning 42–6
friendships
    care plans 107–8
    communication 65
    disclosure 137, 138
    key areas for support 32
    social interaction 67, 68, 69, 72
    support needs 18
    understanding the nature of ASD 27,
        28
further education 143–5

Gantt charts 45
gastric disorders 37, 85
girlfriends 74, 75, 78 see also sex
Grandin, Temple 19, 94

Hampshire, Susan 178
Hawking, Stephen 18, 19
health 84–97
    care plans 111
    case studies 86–90
    key areas for support 32, 33
    organization 37
    physical health 84–6
    psychological obsessions 95–7
    psychological stress 90–5
heat 84
higher education 143–5
Holliday Willey, Liane 35
home management 172–3
honesty 59
housework 48–9, 115
housing see accommodation
human rights 178, 179

identity cards 153, 172
idioms 54, 58
illness 41, 85
imaginative play 12
interpretation 47–51
    establishing connections 47–50

key areas for support 31, 32
    maintaining the connections 50–1
interviews 147, 148, 157
invalidity benefits 150
irony 54
irritable bowel syndrome 85
isolation 68, 173

Kanisza's triangle 23–4
Kanner, Leo 11, 164
Keller, Helen 18

language skills 11, 52, 53 see also
    communication
learning 51, 55
learning support advisors 26, 27, 144
Leather, C. 19
leisure time 110
listening 56–61
literal meanings 58
loneliness 68, 173
lying 59

management role 116–7
marriage 62
McLoughlin, D. 19
meals see diet
media 152, 178
meetings 56, 60, 118, 126
Mencap 161
mental hospitals 121, 157, 158, 162
menus 36, 110
microwaves 38
mimicry 53
Missing Link Support Services 189
money see finances
monitoring 116–7
Morrell, M. 78

Nash, John Forbes 76
National Autism Association 189
National Autistic Society
    contact details 189
    Criminal Justice System 153, 154
    employment 146, 150
    networks 136
    understanding the nature of ASD 22
networks 135–7
neurotypicals (NTs)
    communication 58
    definition of ASD 14, 177
    education 142
    health 91
    interpretation 48, 50
    key areas for support 33
    organization 41
    understanding the nature of ASD 23
noise 93, 151, 154
non-verbal communication
    communication 55, 61, 63, 64, 65
    definition of autism 11
    health 88
    key areas for support 31
    social interaction 70
NTs see neurotypicals

obsessions 95–7, 103, 130, 146
obsessive compulsive disorder (OCD) 38
organization 35–46
    care plans 111
    forward planning 42–6
    instilling order 35–9
    key areas for support 31, 32
    managing change 39–42
    social interaction 67
Orwell, George 178
outreach services 172

pain 84, 85, 111
Palmer, Ann 78
parents 58, 59, 101, 124, 136
part-time work 150
phobias 86, 93
planning
    care plans 114
    family support 126–7
    interpretation 47
    managing support 101–3
    organization 36, 42–6
    support needs 19
police
    care plans 108
    Criminal Justice System 153, 154,
        156, 157, 162
    family support 130
    health 87, 95
praise 50, 55, 82
prison 121, 157, 158
professional support
    accessing services and benefits 166
    disclosure 138
    family support 124, 125, 126, 128
    health 91
    key areas for support 33, 34
    managing support 101, 102, 104
    networks 135
    organization 37
    social interaction 73
    support needs 18, 20
Prospects 150

Rainman 11
rape 76, 77
reading 53
record-keeping 115
registers 154, 172
relationship counselling 74–5
Research Autism 157–8, 189
residential support 173–4
reviews 117–8
rights 44, 178, 179
risk assessments 107
Rogers, Richard 178
role models 178
rotas 115
routines
    care plans 109–10, 115
    employment 146
    family support 123
    health 94
    interpretation 50

organization 36–7, 38, 39, 40, 41,
    42

school
    communication 62
    Criminal Justice System 161
    education 140, 141, 142, 143
    employment 151
    health 86, 87
    networks 136
    social interaction 69
secure mental units 158, 162, 163
self-esteem 50, 81, 88
self-harm 113
sensory overload
    communication 54
    Criminal Justice System 154, 156
    employment 147
    health 93
    organization 44
    social interaction 79
sex 155, 156, 174
Shaw Trust 151, 152, 166
sheltered accommodation 90, 173, 175
shopping 36, 49, 110
siblings 89, 124
sleep patterns 37, 94, 130
social interaction 67–83
    anti-social behaviour 78–83
    communication 59, 63, 64
    coping strategies 70–4
    definition of ASD 11, 13
    difference 67–70
    disclosure 137
    education 144
    employment 149
    key areas for support 32, 33
    networks 135
    sex 74–8
    understanding the nature of ASD 27
social security 150
social workers 92
special educational needs 12, 141, 143
Special Educational Needs and Disability
    Act 2001 (SENDA) 143
specialists 103–4, 128, 157, 159
special schools 140
speech 53, 157
'squeeze machine' 94
stimming 94
stomach problems 37, 85
stranger danger 55
stress
    anti-social behaviour 79, 81
    care plans 111, 112–3, 116
    Criminal Justice System 154, 156,
        158, 159
    education 143
    employment 150
    family support 123
    health 90–5
    key areas for support 32
    managing support 104
    organization 37, 38, 39
Stringer, P. 19
suicide 34, 146

supervision 174
support
    key areas for support 31–4
    managing support 101–4
    organization 35
    philosophy and principles 17–21
    support needs 17–8, 19, 20, 21,
        177
    vision for effective support 171–6
support networks 135–7
support profiles 180–4
support workers
    family support 124, 127, 128
    health 91
    high-level support 174, 175
    interpretation 48
    key areas for support 33, 34
    organization 37, 38, 40
    social interaction 73
surgery 164, 171–2

talents 19, 21
teasing 62, 69, 72, 126, 137
technology 164
temperature 84, 85
theory of mind 12
tick charts 116
time 57
tone of voice 54, 63, 68, 157
transition plans 136
truth telling 59

uncertainty 43
UN Convention on the Rights of Persons
    with Disabilities 178
unemployment 146
United Nations 178, 179
university
    disclosure 137
    education 143
    health 91
    key areas for support 32
    organization 40, 43
    sex 78
    understanding the nature of ASD 26,
        27, 28

video links 154
violence 156
visual impairment 144
visual planners 45
voluntary work 150

waiting 57
Warhol, Andy 178
washing clothes 35, 47, 122
Williams, Donna 22, 43, 50, 81, 94
witnesses 154
work placements 147, 148 see also
    employment
World Health Organization 22

young offenders institutes 158